WALTER DE LA MARE

WALTER DE LA MARE

A CRITICAL STUDY

BY

FORREST REID

NEW YORK

HENRY HOLT AND COMPANY

Republished, 1970
Scholarly Press, 22929 Industrial Drive East
St. Clair Shores, Michigan 48080

MADE AND PRINTED IN GREAT BRITAIN
BY BUTLER & TANNER LIMITED
FROME AND LONDON

Library of Congress Catalog Card Number: 73-131813
Standard Book Number 403-00700-3

TO
J. N. HART

NOTE

I WISH to express my gratitude to Messrs. Longmans, Green, and Company, Messrs. Constable and Company, and Messrs. W. Collins Sons and Company for their courtesy in allowing me to quote from those works in verse and prose by Mr. de la Mare which they publish; also to Mr. J. W. Mackail, the Trustees of the late William Morris, and Messrs. Longmans, Green, and Company for permission to use *Palm Sunday* from Mr. Mackail's *Life of William Morris*; to Mr. H. Caldwell Cook for *The Cloud*, from *Perse Playbooks No.* 2; and to Senator W. B. Yeats for *The Old Men admiring themselves in the Water*, from *Poems* 1899–1905.

F. R.

CONTENTS

ILLUSTRATIONS

AND IF THOU vouchsafe to read this treatise, it shall seem no otherwise to thee, than the way to an ordinary traveller, sometimes fair, sometimes foul; here champaign, there inclosed; barren in one place, better soil in another: by woods, groves, hills, dales, plains, &c. I shall lead thee *per ardua montium, et lubrica vallium, et roscida cespitum, et glebosa camporum,* through variety of objects, that which thou shalt like and surely dislike.—*The Anatomy of Melancholy.*

CHAPTER I

INTRODUCTORY

Such a biographical introduction as one
may prefix to the study of a living author's
work is rarely of much significance. His life
is private, and if his readers are curious to learn
about his childhood, boyhood, and youth, he
alone has a right to gratify that interest. A
great deal of Mr. de la Mare's work is the
creation of a mind brooding upon its earthly
pilgrimage, but, though the material of autobiography may be there, it has been translated
by imagination into poetry or fiction, and
mingled with much that had its origin in the
imagination alone. In all his writings I can
recall only this one brief 'note' from actuality,
which occurs in an article on *Books and Reading*, written in 1919.

Among my early—though not my very earliest—recollec-
tions is that of a far-away Christmas morning. Whether
frost-bound was the air, whether snowflakes were silently
drifting across the window, I cannot remember. But I can

very easily descry—in a vague spectral fashion can even
again become—the small boy of six or seven I then was.
He is sitting up in bed, his wits still fringed with dream,
and in the folds of his counterpane lie an orange, a red-
cheeked apple, a threepenny bit, and a limp stocking that
has well served Santa Claus's purpose.   It is not, however,
the orange or the apple or the threepenny bit that incarnadines
the occasion, but a Book: a limp, broad picture-book, printed
in bold type, with half a dozen or so full-page plates in the
primary colours—Gulliver, pinned down by lank strands of
his hair and being dragged along by a team of cart-horses,
fifty strong, on a vast shallow dray with wheels like reels
of cotton; Gulliver entertaining (and being richly entertained
by) two sneezing Lilliputians in his gold snuff-box; Gulliver
with desperate head just emerging from a Brobdingnagian
bowl of cream.

Not only is it possible to re-animate these glossy and
gaudy pictures more vividly (and with more pleasure) than
to visualize, say, the façade of Buckingham Palace, but with
a ghostly thrill I remember how I then and there proceeded
to spell out word by word that bowdlerized edition of a
romance, which may or may not be the more valuable for
being also a satire, of a satire which is at any rate sacks full
of moidores and doubloons the richer for being also a romance.
Gulliver's Travels, then, was that small boy's first remember-
able book.   In that minute the most insidious of life's habits
had taken this innocent in its nets; the ichor of fantasy had
begun to thin his blood.   He had become—and will probably remain to his last hour—the slave of the printed word.

It was indeed a crucial moment.   What manner of man,
he fondly speculates, would he have been to-day if he had
remained, as he was born, illiterate?

If this whole chapter could be written in

that manner it would indeed be well, but since it cannot I shall rely on brevity, merely supplying a few names and dates.

Walter John de la Mare was born on the 25th of April, 1873, at Charlton in Kent. There is both Scottish and French blood in him. His mother was Scotch (she was the daughter of Dr. Colin Arrot Browning, a naval surgeon), but his father, James Edward de la Mare, was descended from an old Huguenot family. When the boy was four years old the father died and the family removed from Charlton.

It is at this point that autobiography would prove invaluable, for the first secret unfolding of a temperament throws an extraordinary illumination on all that is to follow. The impressions of a child are profound, and one knows that this particular child must have been unusually observant and sensitive. There is much in his work that strikes us as 'remembered', and if several of his small heroes are brought very early face to face with experience, are infinitely more aware of the problems and difficulties of life than their elders suspect, that too, we feel, has been remembered. But such bare facts as that Walter de la Mare was educated at St. Paul's Cathedral Choir School, and while there founded and helped to write a magazine, tell us as little as the contents of the magazine itself, which are indistinguishable from the juvenile efforts most of us indulged in at a similar age. He left school when he was sixteen to enter the City Office of the Anglo-American Oil Company, where he remained for the next nineteen years—that is to say, from 1889 till 1908. In his spare time he continued to write, and presently what he wrote began to find its way into print. There are poems and tales buried in ancient files of *The Pall Mall Magazine*, *The Pall Mall Gazette*, *Black and White*, and *The Sketch*. The first poem is a *Lullaby*, the first stories are *In the Forest*, *Kismet*, and one whose title the author has forgotten. Possibly some of the *Songs of Childhood* were written about this time ; one cannot say, for no notes were ever taken.

Nor do I propose to hark back to these first experiments: I shall begin with certain stories which, though their author has not reprinted them, are definitely stamped with his individuality. Moreover, these particular tales the reader will have little difficulty in turning up should he care to do so. Most libraries contain a run of *The Cornhill Magazine*, and it was in the *Cornhill* they appeared, signed with the author's pseudonym, Walter Ramal.[1]

[1] Dropped after the publication of *Henry Brocken*.

CHAPTER II

REJECTED PROSE (1896–1897)

A MOTE, the first of the tales alluded to, was published in August, 1896, and appended to it was this brief paragraph written by Mr. St. Loe Strachey: 'Those who hold the doctrine of transmigration will hardly fail, after they have read this story, to think that the spirit of Edgar Allan Poe is once more abroad.'

Such a departure from customary editorial taciturnity must have aroused the curiosity of a great many readers. It implied at least that the new story was regarded as something quite out of the common, and whatever one may think of the reference to Poe, there can be no doubt of the enthusiasm which prompted it. As a matter of fact, the comparison will not bear examination, and has been used merely to save the trouble of more precise definition. The name of Poe, in literary shorthand, loosely stands for a kind of story which he himself rarely wrote: a genuine Poe story would be the last in the world to excite an editor's enthusiasm. True, *A Mote* is an excursion into regions of 'the grotesque and arabesque', but the atmosphere, the method of approach, the point of view, are not in the least reminiscent of Poe. The very essence of such tales as *Ligeia*, *Berenice*, *The Black Cat*, *The Fall of the House of Usher*, is a spiritual anguish. They are forced from the writer by some dark, secret collaborator; they are written with the terrible intensity of one who abandons himself to an obsession. They are deliberate in their art, but the impulse behind them is drawn into a certain path by a tormented soul that *must* give expression to what haunts it. *A Mote* is gruesome, fantastic, but it is not a veiled confession, it is not a cry for help; compared with *Berenice* it is the lightest and gayest of fancies. What an editorial note *might* have pointed out is just the absence of any traceable spiritual influence in the new story, its complete originality, not so much of style as of substance. We are conscious of something entirely fresh, distinctly strange, rather whimsical perhaps, and rather baffling. A keen interest is awakened; a difficult thing has been not quite brought off; but it has been sufficiently brought off to excite many conjectures and the liveliest curiosity. The author obviously is still very young, and very preoccupied with his style, which possibly has been influenced by the eclectic theory of R.L.S., and is, at all events, as far removed from the colloquial as he can make it.

Not that there is any resemblance to R.L.S. It is only that, if there are two distinct ideas of style, one of which we may regard as the Stevensonian, and the other as the Wordsworthian, the new writer inclines to the former, which clings as closely to the written, as the latter does to the spoken, word. According to the first idea, style is a thing to be acquired by a process of picking and choosing among models, and the result is an invented idiom into which the natural speech-language of thought and emotion is translated. This, I admit, is more visible in Stevenson's essays than in his tales: still it may be taken as characteristic of his style, and also of George Meredith's. It is often very delightful; it forms part of the charm of *The New Arabian Nights*, and part of the beauty of *The Shaving of Shagpat*: but it is not the best medium for conveying emotion, and sometimes proves quite fatal to that quality. The theory of Wordsworth, on the other hand, is that style must be, or at least appear to be, as natural as breathing—as natural as speech.

Now it seems to me that the prose style of Mr. de la Mare has oddly swayed between these two theories or ideas—here inclining to one, there to the other. The prose of the stories we are at present considering, like the prose of *Henry Brocken*, belongs definitely to class one, but the prose of *The Riddle*, written several years before *Henry Brocken*, belongs equally definitely to class two. So does the prose of *The Return* and of most of the finest short stories, while in certain passages of *The Midget* we see a swaying back (not anything like so marked as in the early tales) towards theory one. Possibly as we proceed what I mean may become clearer.

In these youthful *Cornhill* stories, at any rate, the style is to the last degree literary. Our author likes to drop his adverbial suffixes, to write 'uncommon' where he would have said 'uncommonly': he likes such sentences as 'I was round-eyed at gorgeous birds on the wing': he likes the flavour of quaint obsolete old words that 'act on the fancy like a charm'—likes them nearly as much as Charles Lamb did—and this last liking has survived.

The opening of *A Mote* in conception and even in expression is entirely characteristic of the de la Mare we know.

I awoke from a dream of a gruesome fight with a giant geranium. I surveyed, with drowsy satisfaction and complacency, the eccentric jogs and jerks of my aunt's head. Dozing in her basket chair, she reminded me of an Oriental doll decked in a bunch of gaudy fabrics. Her cap squatted unsafely and awry upon her pendulous curls; her yellow, glossy-skinned, emerald-ringed hands lay loosely upon her silken lap. I sat in my chair like some gorged spider surveying his grey expanse of web, more placid than malevolent concerning this meagre fly. The sleepy sun leered upon the garden with blowzy face. I turned from my aunt to the black cat. The luminous green of his eyes glowered with lazy spitefulness upon the manœuvres of a regiment of gnats. Him too, with sleepy amusement, I wove into the tapestry of my dream.

It would not be difficult, were the piece unsigned, to identify the author of this passage. Aunts, spiders, an observant and rather unaccountable youngster, the method of creating a slightly sinister and wholly strange atmosphere out of commonplace everyday things, of striking the note of a story in its first paragraph by creating a picture that is a kind of symbol of what is to follow—all these idiosyncrasies and technical devices we shall meet with again and again in the later work. But the words that immediately follow those I have quoted betray the writer's immaturity. 'Presently, beyond measure vexed, the beast sprang into the air and buffeted right and left with his fore paws.'

The spell is broken: somehow the conscious turning of the phrase obtrudes itself between the mind's eye and that amazing garden.

Yet, in spite of its failure as a sustained piece of writing, *A Mote* contains so many passages of power and beauty and an uncanny suggestiveness that one would like to see it awarded a place among Mr. de la Mare's canonical works. It really is one of them. Both *Seaton's Aunt* and *Out of the Deep* are unmistakably by the author of *A Mote*. The story is not a tale of terror: the visions of the eccentric Uncle, though terrifying to himself, are too fantastic to produce this effect upon the reader, and the whole thing is composed of these visions, or rather of a series of moving pictures actually projected upon the inside of that queer old man's skull, and which he

watches, literally with inverted eyes. Whence
these pictures come we do not know, but they
form a sequence that seems to image his own
progress through the ages. The minute pilgrim marches on, and around him seethes a
morass of foulness and evil which is somehow
the creation of the watcher himself, who is also,
mysteriously, the pilgrim he watches.

My uncle turned and took my hand. 'And this, Edmond,
this is the man of business . . . the man who courted your
aunt, begot hale and whole children, who sits in his pew and
is respected. That beneath my skull should lurk such mon-
strous things! You are my godchild, Edmond. Actions
are mere sediment, and words—froth, froth. Let the
thoughts be clean, my boy; the thoughts must be clean;
thoughts make the man. You may never at any time be of
ill repute, and yet be a blackguard. Every thought, black
or white, lives for ever, and to life there is no end.'

The weakness of the story, as a story, is not
that it lacks vividness of detail, or colour, or
invention, but that the complete conception
never becomes quite clear. For the most part
we take the thing to be a romantic fantasy,
but there are moments when we ask ourselves if
we are to attach to it an allegorical significance,
if the Uncle's visions represent the slow and
painful evolution of mankind in general. Also
the evil so terrifying to the pilgrim remains

obscure. To be precise, we don't know *what* 'that mote of a man in his black clothes' is suffering, nor why. The logical connexion between the scenes does not come through; there seems to be nothing but an emotion to link them together, such as would suffice in a dream, only this is not a dream story. Sometimes the pictures appear to be symbolical, sometimes to be actual peeps into the past. It is chiefly, then, in its relation to the later work that *A Mote* is so interesting. The choice of a respectable suburban background was exactly right. Arthur Machen and other writers have used the device since, but I do not remember to have come across it earlier, and it is wonderfully effective, partly because of the contrast it affords, and partly because the marvellous, or the merely horrible, becomes much more authentic when it happens, as secretly we should like it to happen, next door.

A Mote, indeed, is so remarkably promising that one is half inclined to doubt if the two stories following it really did follow it. They ought, we feel, to have preceded the earlier tale, for not only is there no advance made but in nearly every respect there is a falling off. *The Village of Old Age* appeared in

September 1896, *The Moon's Miracle* in April 1897; and if *A Mote* does not recall Poe, *The Village of Old Age* does recall Hawthorne. It has so much the appearance of being an allegory—in the manner of the *Mosses from an Old Manse*, or the *Twice-Told Tales*—that to the very end we keep searching for a covert meaning. There is none; it is simply a story; but it is a story such as Henry Brocken might have written, or some youth who had spent all his days shut up in an old-world library. It is languid—more languid than the tale of d'Annunzio's Virgins dying of neglect in their crumbling sun-baked palace—more languid, I think, than anything I have ever read—languid to a point when even the whisper of a dry fluttering leaf would seem a startling noise. And this is intentional; the tone is attuned to the subject; and the subject is decay and death. But the deliberately bookish and archaic style gives it the appearance of a pastiche—spoils it, for when, towards the end, this manner is less rigorously maintained, instantly a faint pallid beauty steals through. It is disappointing; the path the author has chosen we feel can only prove a cul-de-sac; and in the third and longest tale, *The Moon's*

Miracle, the impasse obviously has been reached.

The Moon's Miracle is a description of a battle in the sky fought between the 'nightsmen' and the 'moonsmen' and visible from Wimbledon, whence it is viewed by the Count and his young friend. I don't know whether this sounds a promising subject or not; but the extraordinarily decorative writing accentuates the lack of body in the tale, and its happiest moment is reached when the woman and the street musician, who have nothing to do with it, make their appearance. They are not very real, perhaps, but they are at least less vaporous than the Count and his moonsmen. The bloodless quality noticeable in *The Village of Old Age* —where it was in a way appropriate—removes *The Moon's Miracle* to an arid region of ethereal and ingenious fancy that has no relation whatever to life. Like the refreshingly real Uncle in *A Mote*, Walter Ramal seems to have turned his eyes inward, to be gazing 'under the bows of his eyebones into his own skull', when he should be accumulating impressions of all that is taking place outside and around him. *The Moon's Miracle* must at the time have looked as if it were the end of all things. Fortunately it was but a momentary check, an experiment that was not repeated. When we next encounter our young author it is by no means in the remote regions of astronomical space, but in the midst of human life.

CHAPTER III

SONGS OF CHILDHOOD (1902)

WHAT kind of poetry do children like? One has heard the question asked, and even answered, but since the mind and temperament of a child are as individual as the minds and temperaments of his elders nobody can possibly tell what will sing its way into his spirit, set alight some flame in his imagination. And unless this happens there *is* no poetry, for a poem is a collaboration between the poet and his reader.

What kind of poetry do children write? Except by accident I do not think they write poetry at all, and those interested in the subject must have been struck by the puzzling fact that the accident rarely if ever occurs when the author has passed the age of thirteen. Here is a poem written by a boy of twelve, Master Jack Bitton, which I have taken from the second *Perse Playbook*, published in 1912.

Cloud, O cloud, I love thee,
Streaming across the sky;
Cloud, O cloud, I love thee,
Thou art brilliant to the eye.

And thy great and powerful flight
Doth to our dark hearts bring light;
Rush across the sky with great might,
Then Cloud, O cloud, I love thee.

O cloud, do not rush too fast,
Else thou many dangers pass,
Keep thyself to the very last:
Cloud, O cloud, I love thee.

. . . . . .

My flowers are dying, dying;
Cloud, O cloud, I hate thee:
Listen to a child crying, crying,
Cloud, O cloud, *do* rain.

Clouds are rushing very fast,
Will they give us rain at last?
I can see my own dear cloud
Rushing, rushing, very fast!

Rain has come at last, at last;
Cloud, O cloud, I love thee:
My flowers are reviving fast;
Cloud, O cloud, I love thee.

The rain is gone, and the sun
Is shining very brightly;
Where is my cloud, my own dear one?
O cloud, cloud, I love thee.

This is a child's poem, and the few scattered fragments of poetry I have found in the collection from which it is taken and other similar collections are almost invariably of this kind. Its effect is in great measure due to its immaturity of form. One has the sense of a sort of stammering into speech, and the artlessness of expression, in tune with the simplicity of emotion, is in itself touching—has a beauty that would be extremely difficult to define. The nearest approach to it I have come upon in 'grown-up' poetry is neither in Blake nor in Mr. de la Mare, but in one or two lyrics by William Morris, which he himself never thought worth printing. Here, in *Palm Sunday*, surely sounds the same note of gravity and innocence that gives their fragile charm to the verses I have quoted: it is as if in this lovely thing the voice we can only just overhear in *The Cloud* had become clear and assured.

'Twas in Church on Palm Sunday,
Listening what the priest did say
Of the kiss that did betray,

That the thought did come to me,
How the olives used to be
Growing in Gethsemane.

That the thought upon me came
Of the lantern's steady flame,
Of the softly whispered name.

Of how kiss and words did sound
While the olives stood around,
While the robe lay on the ground.

Then the words the Lord did speak
And that kiss in Holy Week
Dreams of many a kiss did make:

Lover's kiss beneath the moon,
With it sorrow cometh soon:
Juliet's within the tomb:

Angelico's in quiet light
'Mid the aureoles very bright
God is looking from the height.

There the monk his love doth meet:
Once he fell before her feet
Ere within the Abbey sweet

He, while music rose alway
From the Church, to God did pray
That his life might pass away.

There between the angel rows
With the light flame on his brows,
With his friend, the deacon goes:

Hand in hand they go together,
Loving hearts they go together
Where the Presence shineth ever.

Kiss upon the death-bed given,
Kiss on dying forehead given
When the soul goes up to Heaven.

Many thoughts beneath the sun
Thought together; Life is done,
Yet for ever love doth run.

Willow standing 'gainst the blue,
Where the light clouds come and go,
Mindeth me of kiss untrue.

Christ, thine awful cross is thrown
Round the whole world, and thy Sun
Woful kisses looks upon.

.   .   .   .   .   .

Eastward slope the shadows now,
Very light the wind does blow,
Scarce it lifts the laurels low;

I cannot say the things I would,
I cannot think the things I would,
How the Cross at evening stood.

Very blue the sky above,
Very sweet the faint clouds move,
Yet I cannot think of love.

Is *Palm Sunday* then an ideal example of
poetry for children? *All* poetry not beyond
their understanding is poetry for children: by
which I mean for those particular children in
whose natures the seeds of that love have been

[31]

implanted pre-natally. For poetry, of the kind I am approaching, is, I think, either a passion or it is nothing. It cannot come to life, cannot reach us, except in and through a state of emotional and spiritual excitement. It is true there is more than one kind of poetry (though one name has to cover all), and there is a kind in relation to which 'liking' expresses accurately enough the quality of our responsiveness. It is the same, for that matter, with prose. We may very well like *Pride and Prejudice*, but if we only like *Wuthering Heights*, does not that really mean we have missed it? Probably some such idea lies behind Joubert's dictum that 'nothing is poetry which does not transport'; and if the generalization is inadmissible, it is not because the capacity to be transported by a given poem must vary with every reader, but because there really is a type of poem which in no circumstances can we imagine as transporting *anybody*.

> Why so pale and wan, fond lover?
>   Prithee, why so pale?
> Will, when looking well can't move her,
>   Looking ill prevail?
>   Prithee, why so pale?

The lines are graceful, gay, charming—who

will deny that they are poetry? Who, on the
other hand, will affirm that they mean anything
more than precisely what they say, and is what
they say of a nature to transport us? We are
delighted by their urbane wittiness and good-
humour, their distinction, or if you like perfection, of manner. But when Blake writes:

> O Rose, thou art sick!
> The invisible worm,
> That flies in the night,
> In the howling storm,
>
> Has found out thy bed
> Of crimson joy;
> And his dark secret love
> Does thy life destroy.

—though he may indeed only be writing of
a rose growing in a garden, yet with the
very first words a mysterious under-meaning
whispers up out of the depths, gripping our
imagination, throwing open every door and
window to vision and dream. It must be
obvious, then, that this poetry is different in
kind from Suckling's, as different in kind as
Wuthering Heights is from *Pride and Prejudice*.
But it is not, I think, different in kind, but only
in degree, from *The Cloud*. *The Sick Rose* is

C

poetry for children; Suckling's song from
Aglaura is not. Suckling's poem, it seems to
me, might have been written by a man of
talent, Blake's only by a man of genius. And
it is the work of genius—Blake's poem, not
Suckling's; *Wuthering Heights*, not *Pride and
Prejudice*—that depends so much upon the
reader, that can blossom only in a favourable
soil, that is either a miracle or nothing. The
intellect here is the sleepiest of partners; the
imagination of the child may grasp what eludes
the mature intelligence. It would be difficult
to conceive of anybody *more* intelligent than
Henry James was, yet he could write of Poe's
'valueless verse', because for him it really had
no value.

It is at any rate this poetry of imagination
and vision, with its hints of a loveliness belong-
ing to a world perhaps remembered, perhaps
only dreamed, but which at least is not *this*
world, that will be the subject of our present
essay. Mr. de la Mare has written little else.
His last poetry may be infinitely deeper than
his first, but it remains the same in kind.

In the beginning it is simple and untroubled,
seeking no more than to lull us into dreamland.

I had a silver buckle,
I sewed it on my shoe,
And 'neath a sprig of mistletoe
I danced the evening through!

I had a bunch of cowslips,
I hid 'em in a grot,
In case the elves should come by night
And me remember not.

I had a yellow riband,
I tied it in my hair,
That, walking in the garden,
The birds might see it there.

I had a secret laughter,
I laughed it near the wall:
Only the ivy and the wind
May tell of it at all.

I have quoted *The Buckle* in its first form, because the change of 'I hid 'em in a grot' to 'I hid them in a grot' seems to me mysteriously to remove some of its virtue from that line. The original line, in its rapidity, suggests the quickness and eagerness of the little girl moving about her garden. But I quote the poem especially for the sake of the last stanza, in which the garden is suddenly flooded with a light from the shores of an eternal childhood.

I had a secret laughter,
I laughed it near the wall. . . .

[35]

Why do these words produce a slight shock of surprise and recognition? I cannot tell: I do not suppose the poet himself always knows where such things come from. And for that reason it is dangerous to tamper with early work. To take the trifling instance of the changed line I have mentioned; may it not have been that when it was first written the writer had before him the particular picture it calls up in his reader's mind, but when he came back to it, years afterwards, this picture did not happen to recur, and the line was altered to suit another mood? Such a theory, in relation to a couple of dropped letters, may appear far-fetched in the extreme: none the less I believe it to be founded on a truth.

Songs of Childhood was issued in 1902. It was a very secret performance, as first books often are, only the poet's mother and one or two friends knowing anything about it till it was actually published. Whether the manuscript was sent to more than one publisher I do not know, but, first or last, it was Andrew Lang who 'discovered' and accepted it for Messrs. Longmans. Whatever may be our opinion of Lang's taste in fiction, which seems all his life to have remained more or less what it had been in his schooldays, his feeling for poetry was delicate and true. His devotion to Homer did not prevent him from writing charmingly of both Edgar Poe and Gérard de Nerval at a time when it was less common to praise these poets than it is now, and what he admired he took a good deal of trouble to bring to the notice of others. His reception of the *Songs of Childhood* was extraordinarily kind: the typescript with his pencilled notes and comments on the individual poems still exists to prove it.

It must have been a singularly pleasant task, the first reading of that manuscript. To-day the work of Mr. de la Mare is famous; his outlook, his world, his choice of subject, his manner, are familiar to us; but I can myself remember when this was not so: I can remember a winter afternoon many years ago, in the University Library at Cambridge, when I was prowling round the shelves upstairs and took down by the merest chance a thin pale-blue volume called *Songs of Childhood*, by Walter Ramal. I had never heard of Walter Ramal, and the book opened at this poem:

'Sailorman, I'll give to you
My bright silver penny,
If out to sea you'll sail me
And my dear sister Jenny.'

I don't know if my reader will have had a similar experience, and I cannot now from the *Songs of Childhood* itself quite recapture it, but it was as if in the silence and fading light of that deserted library, I had, like some adventurer in the Middle Ages, sailed all unexpectedly into sight of an unknown and lovely shore. Apart from everything else, there was this thrill of a complete newness. I read on and on. I hunted in the catalogue for other books by Walter Ramal. He had written one other, *Henry Brocken.* In the meantime, on my way back to my rooms, I ordered this book, and got it two days later. Thus it was that for many years *Songs of Childhood* held a kind of jealous place in my affections—even up till the publication of *The Listeners* and *Peacock Pie*—for an impression so vivid is hard to dislodge. It still seems to me a marvellous first book, filled with a romantic beauty, innocent and happy even in its more pensive moments. Moreover, its beauty has proved lasting, and we can, I think, find in it the first hints and stirrings of a great deal that has followed. It is too easy to call it fantastic, for when all is said one of its rarest qualities is its truth. We can, in fact, just as if we were criticizing a short story, say that the child in these poems lives. It is this living child, yielding to that streak of a darker curiosity so characteristic of him, who stands stockstill, rooted in his path, while he stares in fascination at the rats running over John Mouldy in his cellar—appalled, delighted.

> I spied John Mouldy in his cellar,
>   Deep down twenty steps of stone;
> In the dusk he sat a-smiling,
>   Smiling there alone.
>
> He read no book, he snuffed no candle;
>   The rats ran in, the rats ran out;
> And far and near, the drip of water
>   Went whispering about.
>
> The dusk was still, with dew a-falling,
>   I saw the Dog Star bleak and grim,
> I saw a slim brown rat of Norway
>   Creep over him.

It is horrible and it is beautiful, and the beauty is like a flickering zigzag play of lightning by which we see the horror. There is a stark intensity in its realism. Nothing could be more gruesome than the whispering water unless it be that slim brown rat of Norway. And then, suddenly, with the first two lines of the third stanza, the cold pure beauty of the sky at nightfall arches above us.

John Mouldy comes closer to the mature work of Mr. de la Mare than anything else in the volume. It is all his, while a few of the other poems betray to a slight extent the influence of his reading. For that reason I should place *The Pedlar* among the very earliest:

> There came a pedlar to an evening house;
> Sweet Lettice, from her lattice looking down,
> Wondered what man he was, so curious
> His black hair tangled on his tattered gown:
> Then lifts he up his face with glittering eyes,—
> 'What will you buy, sweetheart?—Here's honeycomb,
> And mottled pippins, and sweet mulberry pies,
> Comfits and peaches, snowy cherry bloom,
> To keep in water for to make night sweet;
> All that you want, sweetheart,—come, taste and eat!'

There is something of de la Mare in it, but there is more of Keats and of Christina Rossetti. And is there not a delightfully familiar ring about the opening of *this* poem?

> How large unto the tiny fly
> Must little things appear!

Only for a moment, however, does our fly recall the divine and moral busy bee; the echo dies out at once; he has no lesson to teach us, but sits there in Epicurean aloofness, waiting for the thoughtful Maria.

There are poems which are hardly more than strains of music:

> O for a heart like almond boughs!
>   O for sweet thoughts like rain!
> O for first-love like fields of grey
> Shut April-buds at break of day!
>   O for a sleep like music!
>   Dreams still as rain! [1]

—there are poems which are hardly more than nursery nonsense:

> Here are crocuses, white, gold, grey!
>   'O dear me!' says Marjorie May;
> Flat as a platter the blackberry blows:
>   'O dear me!' says Madeleine Rose;
> The leaves are fallen, the swallow flown:
>   'O dear me!' says Humphrey John;
> Snow lies thick where all night it fell:
>   'O dear me!' says Emmanuel.

—there are poems which are pure fantasy, such as *Dame Hickory* and *I Saw Three Witches*: but most of the poems have a story in them. Here is *Sleepyhead*, originally called *The Gnomies*.

[1] The lovely diminuendo of the last line is due to later revision.

WALTER DE LA MARE

As I lay awake in the white moonlight,
I heard a faint singing in the wood—
   'Out of bed,
   Sleepyhead,
  Put your white foot, now;
   Here are we,
   'Neath the tree,
   Singing round the root now!'

I looked out of window in the white moonlight,
The trees were like snow in the wood—
   'Come away
   Child and play,
   Light wi' the gnomies;
   In a mound,
   Green and round,
   That's where their home is!

   'Honey sweet,
   Curds to eat,
   Cream and frumenty,
   Shells and beads,
   Poppy seeds,
   You shall have plenty.'

But soon as I stooped in the dim moonlight
To put on my stocking and my shoe,
The sweet, sweet singing died sadly away,
And the light of the morning peep'd through:
Then instead of the gnomies there came a red robin
To sing of the buttercups and dew.[1]

---

[1] A word as to the reading of this poem.   I prefer to read
the first line as if it were prose—
  As I lay awake in the white moonlight,
letting the lilt begin to sound in the second, before it breaks
into the gay song tune.

This is the first, and I think best, version. Let me dwell for a moment on the picture in it—the shadowy room in which we watch the little boy putting first one foot and then the other down on the dark carpet; yawning, rubbing the sleep from his eyes, tip-toeing to the window, staring out. Then the quick astonished fumbling for shoes and stockings, and the sudden merry interruption of the robin and the morning. And in the last couplet what a lovely suggestion of freshness and coolness and the awakening of life outside the house! It is all homely, simple, and infinitely pleasant, with an innocence not re-captured but natural.

Imagination is the power by which we grasp reality. An imaginative man is less a dreamer than a seer. It is when the imagination weakens that we sink into dream. That is why Blake, in whom the imagination is all-powerful, is never dreamy, but always definite and sure; and that is why the children in these poems are so living to us that we know what they look like, know their names and their ages, the colour of their eyes and hair, even their clothes. We know that the child in *The Buckle* is a nimble, elfin, little creature; we know that Jane is

[43]

plump and often rather hot, and that she usually carries her hat swinging by its brim instead of wearing it properly on her head. We know that the slimmer, taller, more sophisticated Elaine is flaxen-haired, delicate-skinned, and wears a cool-tinted muslin dress and long black stockings that never get into wrinkles. And I protest this is not fanciful, not made up for the occasion. If, as Coleridge says, 'the power of poetry is, by a single word perhaps, to instil that energy into the mind which compels the imagination to produce the picture,' then already, in these earliest poems, we find this power constantly in evidence. The very names contribute their share to the illusion, their fitness is not due to happy chance.

> When slim Sophia mounts her horse
> And paces down the avenue. . . .

—call the girl by any other name—Priscilla, Miranda, Jemima, Rebecca—and the picture will be different. Even the metre in which the poem is written moves with a curiously liquid tune that follows the measured pacing of the horse.

But it is the more fantastic poems whose charm is so individual. Here we have, what is always to remain characteristic of the author, the clearest, most exact and detailed painting of earthly beauty, mingled with an unearthly and spiritual beauty. The vision is closely akin to the absorbed, penetrating, wonder-working vision of childhood, though there is something added which comes from experience. But beauty and vision are as yet untinged by mysticism, are almost exclusively a matter of light and colour and atmosphere.

> In the black furrow of a field
> I saw an old witch-hare this night;
> And she cocked her lissome ear,
> And she eyed the moon so bright,
> And she nibbled o' the green;
> And I whispered 'Whsst! witch-hare,'
> Away like a ghostie o'er the field
> She fled and left the moonlight there.[1]

It will be seen that we are in a world as uncertain as that Thessaly—birth-place of magic —where the bewildered Lucius nervously picked his way till at last 'Not an object did I see but I straightway took it to be something

[1] Again, if it is not impertinent, I should like to make a suggestion as to reading: that in line six the reader should leave a longish pause between 'Whsst!' and 'witch-hare', with another pause after 'hare'. Then the rapid scamper of the last two lines becomes the hare's own flight.

else. Stones, birds, trees, fountains—in everything I saw unfortunate human creatures transformed by fatal words.' So it is with poor Lucy when she goes 'a-walking', and with Jane and with Ann. They are ready to start at a mouse, to find a wolf behind every bush, a ghost behind every door, a witch in every crow. But the little boy in the story cannot have too many adventures.

> I saw three witches
> Asleep in a valley,
> Their heads in a row, like stones in a flood,
> Till the moon, creeping upward,
> Looked white through the valley,
> And turned them to bushes in bright scarlet bud.

It is all deliciously exciting; he never knows what will happen next; the oddest things are happening every minute: in fact—from the moment he wakes in the morning and peeps out of his window, till, tired and sleepy, he turns his back on a land of marvels—this inveterate explorer is 'present always at the focus where the greatest number of vital forces unite', not only 'in their purest energy', but in the most perplexing fashion. And when the adventures are over, the ogre is gone 'whinnying down the dale', the wolf is routed, the

[46]

witches are once more only 'three crows upon a bough'—then follows the instinctive reaction at the end of a long, crowded day—the desire to let himself sink back into the quiet comforting assurance of what he knows and loves.

> Sleep, sleep, lovely white soul;
> The little mouse cheeps plaintively,
> The night-bird in the chestnut-tree—
> They sing together, bird and mouse,
> In starlight, in darkness, lonely, sweet,
> The wild notes and the faint notes meet—
>   Sleep, sleep, lovely white soul.
>
> Sleep, sleep, lovely white soul;
> Time comes to keep night-watch with thee,
> Nodding with roses; and the sea
> Saith 'Peace! Peace!' amid his foam.
> 'O be still!'
> The wind cries up the whispering hill—
>   Sleep, sleep. . . .

It is doubtful if a small reader will quite realize the full beauty of that 'O be still!', whose music, in its sudden pause, falls on the ear as with a passionate tenderness. It is doubtful, I say, for who can tell through what subconscious channels such things may not reach a child's mind? All we can hazard is that the child in the book is not collaborating here, that the closing words are left to the other, who looks on, looks back.

In these poems, of course, we find only the dawn of Mr. de la Mare's genius. Much will be added, much will be developed; but this first clear youthful note possesses its own appropriate beauty. The writer outgrew his book, became dissatisfied with it, attempted to bring it into closer harmony with his later work, or perhaps one should say with his later technique. The attempt was interesting and not very happy. One gets from it an odd impression that he has lost touch with this beginner, is not trying to help him in *his* way, but wants to make him different: in fact it is almost like a case of imperfect sympathy. Some of the poems are dropped, some expanded, some altered nearly out of recognition. A few new ones are added—the delightful *Funeral* among them, which should not be, as it is in the *Collected Poems*, dated 1901, since in mood and form it belongs clearly to the *Peacock Pie* group. The various editions are, however, worth examining in detail.

There are at present three distinct texts of *Songs of Childhood*. There is the original text

[48]

of 1902 (the date is wrongly given as 1901 in the *Collected Poems*), there is the revised text of 1916, and there is what I suppose we may call the definitive text—that of the aforesaid *Collected Poems*, published in two volumes in 1920. Meanwhile text number two continues to be printed in Longmans' edition of *Songs of Childhood*: that is to say, if you now buy *Songs of Childhood* as a separate book, it is text number two you get.

But it is text number two that is so different. The first and third texts differ, but not nearly so much as the first and second, many of the original versions having been restored in 1920. Thus the *Sleepyhead* of 1920 is very nearly identical with *The Gnomies* of 1902: but the *Sleepyhead* of 1916 is practically a new poem. I give it in full.

> As I lay awake in the white moon light,

(the splitting of moonlight into two words makes it here almost necessary to read 'As I lay awake | in the white | moon light'—rhyming 'white' with 'light', a jingle to my own ear unpleasant).

> As I lay awake in the white moon light,
> I heard a faint singing in the wood,

[49]   D

'Out of bed,
Sleepyhead,
Put your foot and come away;
Clear peeps the moonbeam,
Abloom is the may;
Leave your sleep and with the fairies
Come, child, and play!'

I looked out of window, in the white moon light,
The leaves were like snow in the wood—
'Listen, O listen,
Music is falling;
Tiny lanterns clash and glisten;
Voices are calling;
Far, far the blue air shakes;
Hov'ring and winging,
Float we in light and shadow,
Singing—singing.'

Softly I stooped in the dim moon light
To put on my stocking and my shoe,
But the sweet shrill singing echoed faintly away,
And the grey of the morning peeped through,
And the voices that called me were blackbird and robin,
Astir in the twilight and dew.

The whole poem is altered; a freshness and gaiety are gone out of it, and, for me, my picture is lost. How can there be a dark carpet since it was created by Sleepyhead's white foot, which is no longer white?—and the carpet seems to have made the room, and the room the tip-toeing to the window. The scene, the movement, the life, **have** strangely faded: I might trace the altered significance from line to line —on to the last couplet, which leaves us still in twilight, while what was charming in the original ending was that morning awakened in it.

> Then instead of the gnomies there came a red robin
> To sing of the buttercups and dew.

Is it not for that matter truer:—truer, that is to say (in a sort of careless lightheartedness in it), to this little chap who is telling us the story?

The only excuse for these comments, however, is the extraordinary interest of the variants; for the author, as I have said, has in most cases restored the earlier versions. But this second text really differs so considerably from the first and third that the student of Mr. de la Mare's work will naturally desire to possess it. I shall leave him, then, to make all further comparisons for himself, merely pointing out here omissions and additions where entire poems are concerned.

The 'songs' of 1902 omitted from the 1916 book are *The Night Swans*, *The Grey Wolf*, *Cecil*, and *Envoy*. As well as these four, two further poems disappear in the *Collected Poems* of 1920—namely, *O Dear Me!* and *The Child in the Story Awakes*, the former of which I have quoted on an earlier page. The new poems of 1916 are *A-tishoo* (omitted in 1920), *The Rainbow*, *The Fiddlers* (omitted in 1920), *The Funeral*, and *Envoy*—not the *Envoy* of 1902, but a new and much better poem. The poems which have been most altered in the process of revision are *The Pilgrim*, *The Phantom*, *Down-Adown-Derry*, and *The Isle of Lone*. The absence from both later collections of the amusing and very characteristic *Grey Wolf* is puzzling, because it is among the most successful of the lighter pieces.

CHAPTER IV

HENRY BROCKEN (1904)

HENRY BROCKEN, the first of Mr. de la Mare's prose romances, was written on the note-paper of the Anglo-American Oil Company. Shall we let the author himself describe his book in an Introduction composed for it though never printed?

Whether or not other eyes than mine will ever look upon this little book, I cannot say, nor hardly care to inquire. I consign it to the river-water, somewhat better at ease and conscience, but yet anxious lest it fall into the hands of the profane, who might care so little for the peace and beauty of these strange lands as to attempt to come hither.

Nevertheless perhaps there is little cause for my fears. Men of nowadays love smoke and clatter and what they call prosperity better than to risk anything at the mere idle tale of a traveller. If, indeed, I had entered the gates of Paradise itself, it is little likely my account of it, however well-established its publishers, however learned its editor, however sage its reviewers, would persuade any person to win thither for himself. It is an old story—almost past a jest.

I have therefore determined to keep silence where silence seems best. I present no chart, I recite neither latitude nor longitude, I will but describe as best I can the land to which Happy Chance has conducted me, and wherein it seems Happy Chance means to keep me.

One thing, however, I will say with all gravity. No traveller is welcome here that comes not with an open heart, at least the remembrance of childhood in his mind, and a pocket careless whether it be full or empty. All I find are in some wise children here. None is the slave of habit, none of withered fact. Bohemia may quite easily become a seaport here, and never a wiseacre will so much as blink his eyes. Here often sprouts mistletoe upon the oak. I have seen hoarfrost upon the wild roses, and the moon rise full four nights running, yet never a whit dimmed in silver by so much lawless toil, nor weary of calling to the waters. Birds I have heard, strange to summer, sing among the linden tassels, and once even the cuckoo called hollowly cuck-oo to me across a pool thick and still with ice and banked with untrodden snow.

And again, as for an open heart. One might as well hope to see with shut eyes as understand without an open heart in these regions. It is not indeed what is seen but who sees it that matters much in the few flashy years of life and in what men call actuality. As again it is not what is credible but who is credulous that keeps the faggots busy and man a little above the beasts.

There remains then only the careless pocket. In this country so far as I have seen only fairy gold is current coin. Offer a flat plate of the precious metal with a flattish head stamped upon it, how flatly it is disdained. There is better gold in running water they seem to think. While for silver and bronze—are there not little birch leaves and lichens upon tombs?

Thus then I think I shall dissuade most of the profane from venturing hither, even I dare say from wasting their

time in reading my book. Very heartily I bid them fare-
well. Parallel lines are such it is said as never can by any
possibility meet. Would to God then we be in future quite
parallel.

There remains that little company I care for and venture
my book to; and towards them I look with a very weak
courage and perplexed eyes. I know full well how poor
a pen one may possess concurrently with a sanguine and
eager heart. The spirit often flags that alone can make
alive, the word comes not that would tell duly. But love
remains.

Let me then ask very humbly pardon once for all. Some
perhaps who read of the personages that cross these pages
are already familiar with them face to face. They will have
nothing but contempt for such poor shadows of them as I
shall conjure up. So be it. I can but do my best to say
the thing that *is*, as my friend, Mr. Gulliver would say; and
if my honesty swears it my best, I can no other.

This, it seems to me, gives a very just
account of a charming but uneven composition,
which occupies a place rather less than halfway
between the early experimental prose and the
tales that are to follow it. *Henry Brocken*, also,
is an experiment. For a *story* it is overloaded
with picture; but, except in one or two chapters
which stand clearly apart from the rest, the
author's purpose seems to hover between criticism and creation. The writing often possesses
great beauty, but is still marred at times by a
decoration that draws attention to the surface

and away from the content. It is always best where it is simplest, and it is always simplest where the appeal of the subject is less intellectual than emotional.

'And by-and-by we came to a house called Gloom, whose gardens slope down with plashing fountains and glimmering banks of flowers into the shadow and stillness of a broad valley. . . .' The house, the garden, rise up softly and darkly from the white printed page. But when we turn to the next page and read, 'He seemed a man Mars lends to Venus out of war to unhappy idleness,' illusion dies on the instant.

Taken as a whole, the book lacks the freshness, and above all the reality, of *Songs of Childhood*. Is it because it is in prose; because at this time Mr. de la Mare's verse style is better than his prose style (such a sentence as I have quoted would be impossible in *Songs of Childhood*)? Is it because of its length, or because of its theme? I am inclined to answer 'yes' to all three questions. Certainly *Henry Brocken* is worthy of its place among the author's works, among his juvenilia: it is a genuine first-fruit, his genius is in it, though hampered by the nature of the task he has undertaken. It may seem rash to say that the subject does not suit him, for the subject is poetry, yet I cannot help saying so. The subject is poetry, but it is other people's poetry; the moment he has a chance to make his own poetry the whole thing is lifted on to a different plane. The first three pages provide as fascinating an opening to a romance as could be desired; on the fourth we pass out of the world which is the author's own world, and do not catch again more than a fleeting glimpse of it till Henry, escaping from the palace of the Sleeping Beauty, plunges into the torrent that carries him to the country of the Houyhnhnms. In the interval much of the book is like a whispering gallery where we listen to the voices of dead poets. There is no attempt to bring the hero to a more active life than is necessary for the conveying of a mood of reverie. Henry Brocken, the young bookworm, is far less real to us than his old mare Rosinante. This gentle, ambling creature is indeed an equine heroine of remarkable charm; but Henry remains a phantom of the same consistency as the ghosts he encounters. We do not even know whether he is man or boy. When we try to look at him we see no more than the mirrored image of the country he is riding through, or of its inhabitants, and these images themselves are subdued, softened, by the perpetual twilight floating in his soul. We know of him only that he has been left by his Aunt Sophia to pass a solitary childhood and boyhood in a well-stocked library, that one morning he rides out on the broad back of Rosinante in search of adventure, and that the library accompanies him. Its walls have dissolved, its shelves have disappeared, it has expanded into a mysterious country-side, but that country-side is peopled with the people of his books. It is like some sleepy meadow of Persephone, haunted by shades who have found no Paradise. Julia, Dianeme, Electra, Anthea, Nick Bottom and Lucy Gray, are little more than voices; even Jane Eyre is strangely passive. It is only where the author has boldly re-drawn his originals that they really come to life. Thus, in the palace of the Sleeping Beauty the spirit of life and adventure begins to stir, and in the land of the Houyhnhnms it is wide awake.

These Gulliver chapters—the seventh and eighth—contain by far the finest creative writing in the book. Taken by themselves

they make an admirable short story, as human
and moving as the rest of the book is remote
and dream-burdened. When we reach them
it is as if we had come out from an insub-
stantial lunary world into the full blaze of day.
It is most curious how the reaction from
Swift's morose pessimism has instilled an energy
into the author's imagination, which Wordsworth, Herrick, Shakespeare, and Charlotte
Brontë left only dreamily acquiescent. Certainly, now for the first time we see it really
taking flight, cleaving the air on its own
strong wings. The power and beauty glowing in these chapters are as tonic as the wind
sweeping across the broad green prairies where
the horses wheel and thunder. All Swift's
values are reversed. The Yahoo is as lovable
a creature as Swift's was hateful, and yet
remains Yahoo. The horses are still glorious
in their strength and beauty, but there is an
obscure patient glory in the spirit of their
slave which they cannot imagine. And it is
our Yahoo, with his dog-like fidelity and devotion, who saves Henry Brocken. The horses
are closing in on them, bent on their destruction:

It was a long and arduous and unequal contest. I wished

very heartily I could bear a rather less passive part. But this fearless creature scarcely heeded me; used me like a helpless child, half tenderly, half roughly, displaying ever and again over his shoulder only a fleeting glance of the shallow glories of his eyes, as if to reassure me of his power and my safety. . . .

Far distant in front of us there appeared to be a break in the level green, a fringe of bushes, a rougher ground. For this refuge he was making, and from this our mutinous Houyhnhnms meant to keep us.

There was no pausing now, not a glance behind. His every effort was bent on speed. Speed indeed it was. The wind roared in my ears. Yet above its surge I heard the neighing and squealing, the ever-approaching shudder of hoofs. . . .

Then, of a sudden, a last shrill paean rose high; the hosts of our pursuers paused, billow-like, reared, and scattered —my poor Yahoo leapt clear.

For an instant once again in this wild journey I was poised, as it were, in space, then fell with a crash, still clutched, sure and whole, to the broad shoulders of my rescuer.

When my first confusion had passed away, I found that I was lying in a dense green glen at the foot of a cliff. For some moments I could think of nothing but my extraordinary escape from destruction. Within reach of my hand lay the creature who had carried me, huddled and motionless; and to left and to right of me, and one a little nearer the base of the cliff, five of the sorrel horses that had been our chief pursuers. One only of them was alive, and he, also, broken and unable to rise—unable to do else than watch with fierce, untamed, glazing eyes (a bloody froth at his muzzle) every movement and sign of life I made.

I myself, though bruised and bleeding, had received no serious injury. But my Yahoo would rise no more. His master was left alone amidst his people. I stooped over him and bathed his brow and cheeks with the water that trickled from the cliffs close at hand. I pushed back the thick strands of matted yellow hair from his eyes. He made no sign. Even while I watched him, the life of the poor beast near at hand welled away; he whinnied softly, and dropped his head upon the bracken. I was alone in the unbroken silence.

This narrative, it seems to me, is superbly conceived and written. It has an uplifting quality, a reality, an assured power, that are extraordinarily stimulating. Next in excellence I should place the Bunyan chapters, and, in their so different vein, the few pages that carry us to 'the uttermost shores of Tragedy'.

It was in searching sea and cliff for the least sign of life that I thought I descried on the furthest extremity of the nearer of the horns of the bay the spires and smouldering domes of a little city. If I gazed intently, they seemed to vanish away, yet still to shine above the azure if, raising my eyes, I looked again.

So, caring not how far I must go so long as my path lay beside these breaking waters, I set out on the firm, white sands to prove this city the mirage I deemed it.

What wonder, then, my senses fell asleep in that vast lullaby! And out of a day-dream almost as deep as that in which I first set out, I was suddenly aroused by a light tapping sound, distinct and regular between the roaring breakers.

I lifted my eyes to find the city I was seeking evanished away indeed. But nearer at hand a child was playing upon the beach, whose spade among the pebbles had caused the bird-like noise I had heard.

So engrossed was she with her building in the sand that she had not heard me approaching. She laboured on at the margin of the cliff's shadow where the sea-birds cried, answering Echo in the rocks. So solitary and yet so intent, so sedate and yet so eager a little figure she seemed in the long motionlessness of the shore, by the dark heedlessness of the sea, I hesitated to disturb her.

Who of all Time's children could this be playing uncompanioned by the sea? And at a little distance betwixt me and her in the softly-mounded sand her spade had already scrawled in large, ungainly capitals, the answer—'Annabel Lee.' The little flounced black frock, the tresses of black hair, the small, beautiful dark face—this then was Annabel Lee; and that bright, phantom city I had seen—that was the vanishing mockery of her kingdom.

I called her from where I stood—'Annabel Lee!' She lifted her head and shook back her hair, and gazed at me startled and intent. I went nearer.

'You are a very lonely little girl,' I said.

'I am building in the sand,' she answered.

'A castle?'

She shook her head.

'It was in dreams,' she said, flushing darkly.

'What kind of dream was it in then?'

'Oh! I often dream it; and I build it in the sand. But there's never time: the sea comes back.'

'Was the tide quite high when you began?' I asked; for now it was low.

'Just that much from the stones,' she said; 'I waited for it ever so long.'

'It has a long way to come yet,' I said; 'you will finish it *this* time, I dare say.'

She shook her head and lifted her spade.

'Oh no; it is much bigger, more than twice. And I haven't the seaweed, or the shells, and it comes back very, very quickly.'

'And where is the little boy you play with down here by the sea?'

She glanced at me swiftly and surely; and shook her head again.

'He would help you.'

'He didn't in my dream,' she said doubtfully. She raised long, stealthy eyes to mine, and spoke softly and deliberately. 'Besides, there isn't any little boy.'

Yes, this is Annabel Lee; but is she not more de la Mare's creation than Poe's; might she not, in her 'little flounced black frock', with her 'tresses of black hair' and her 'long, stealthy eyes', have stepped straight out of one of his own tales on to that desolate shore which is Poe's?

Personally I should have liked the journey to have ended here. It really seems to be the ending; but in a last chapter, of which I admit I can make but little, Henry Brocken crosses the sea to the island of the subtle and enigmatic Criseyde.

This then is the story, and it has many beauties, and everywhere a kind of fragrance, though except in the Gulliver chapters, I think, not so much of growing flowers as of

those old-fashioned china jars of dried petals
and spices, familiar objects in the days of one's
childhood, which possessed the delightful prop-
erty of filling winter rooms with the memory
of summer rose gardens.

Henry Brocken is a strange book, and not the
least strange thing about it is that one's impression of it never seems to be final. It is in this
way remarkably like a flesh-and-blood companion, with whom one may quarrel, but to
whom one keeps on returning, because what
one loves and admires so far outweighs what
one dislikes. None of Mr. de la Mare's books
can be judged at a first or even a second
reading, and this one bears the test of many
readings. And none of his books could be
presented in so false a light as this one. It
leaves behind it a 'cloud of witnesses' that rise
unbidden in the mind, a state of hauntedness.
It may be, as one ponders on it, the strange
pale treacherous figure of Prince Ennui, accompanied by his cruel, phantom, milk-white
hounds, that will emerge soundlessly out of
the gloaming; it may be the two boys, Sleep and
Death, who will beckon us to their churchyard
where they sport, naked and lovely, among the
ruinous tombs:

They stayed at a little distance from us with dwelling eyes and parted lips. Then the fairer and, as it seemed to me, elder of the brothers stooped and plucked a few blades of grass and proffered them, half fearfully, to the beast that amazed him. But the other gave less heed to Rosinante, fixed the filmy lustre of his eyes on me, his wonderful young face veiled with that wisdom which is in all children, and of an immutable gravity.

The prevailing mood, as I have said, is reverie—languid at times, but ever and again shot through with sudden brilliant lights of imagination. The languor itself is a sign of youth, of immaturity: it is, at all events, to be found in nothing Mr. de la Mare has written since. The drowsy golden haze that suffuses certain pages of *The Return* is quite unlike it, is warm and rich with life and the promise of life. But in *Henry Brocken* nature herself is spellbound. There are no reapers in the fields, no picnickers in the woods, the rattle and rumble of a country cart never intrudes on the trance-like stillness. The rare sounds are lonely sounds—the breaking of waves on a deserted beach, the solitary call of a wild bird. We are in a dream-world, and at first cock-crow all will dissolve and melt away; Henry Brocken will awaken and find himself back in his library—will blow out his candle

and climb, a little stiffly and with a faint chill
in his blood, up the dark staircase to bed.

And that, I take it, was the author's intention. With the *Ideal Craftsman* of the following year he turns his back on this glimmering,
'cloud-capped' land of reverie, and begins to
build up in prose his own extraordinarily vivid
and living world, just as, in *Songs of Childhood*,
he had already begun to build it in verse.

CHAPTER V

STORIES REVIVED (1900-1909)

IT is here that the chronological plan I had
proposed to adopt in this survey of Mr. de
la Mare's writings becomes difficult and uncertain. The author himself has no note of
when the tales I am now about to discuss
were written. With one exception, they were
first collected in 1923, in the volume called
The Riddle, which also contained a group of
much later stories written about the time the
book was issued. But these earlier stories
belong, some of them, to a period preceding
Songs of Childhood and *Henry Brocken*:—that
is to say, in their first form they belonged to
this period, for they have been revised, and
how much or how little revised I cannot tell
except in the case of *The Riddle* itself.

Of *The Count's Courtship* and *The Almond
Tree*, for instance, though the latter was not
published in *The English Review* till 1909,
the author is sure that in their first shapes they

must have followed closely on the *Cornhill* stories. The Count, it will be remembered, was introduced to us in one of those stories, *The Moon's Miracle*, and since this remarkable person (who figures also in *The Almond Tree*) is hardly likely to have been revived in later years, the date of these three compositions may be regarded as fairly well established. *The Looking Glass* Mr. de la Mare believes to be rather later; but it, *The Bird of Travel*, *The Bowl*, and *Miss Duveen*, are all very early stuff rewritten. *The Riddle*—just as we have it now—appeared in *The Monthly Review* in 1900.

That the rewriting in some cases meant a good deal more than mere verbal revision I feel sure. Were it not for the presence of the Count in it, it would be hard to believe *The Almond Tree* belonged to the same period as *The Moon's Miracle*. One wonders, in fact, how much of the original story really has survived. *The Bird of Travel* and *The Looking Glass* are to my mind the weakest of these early tales; *An Ideal Craftsman* and *The Almond Tree* the richest in content; *The Riddle* and *Miss Duveen* the most perfect.

The direct method employed in the telling

of *The Riddle* was of course much easier than the indirect method of *The Almond Tree*. The beauty of *The Almond Tree*, or one of its beauties, lies in the fact that, as the author saw his subject, form and substance are essentially indivisible. I mean, the treatment in this instance becomes a *part* of the story. The story does not consist of the mere naked happenings in it, but of these happenings coloured, and therefore to some extent transformed, by the consciousness of the little boy whose mind is the medium through which they reach us. To put it in a nutshell, the story is the child's incomplete vision of it: it is like a landscape mirrored in an enchanted pool, and much of its richness, beauty, and intensity, springs from the exquisite lights and tones it thus acquires.

It was Henry James in his later work who, consciously at least, first made technique a part of dramatic narrative, and lifted at the same time the whole art of fiction on to a higher plane. One of the differences between a Jacobean novel and an ordinary novel is that the former is written for an ideal reader of responsive yet fastidiously critical intelligence, whereas by most novelists this personage is

regarded as mythical, or at any rate negligible.
But the author of *The Spoils of Poynton* utterly
refused to rely on that robust virtue which
Mr. E. M. Forster in his *Aspects of the Novel*
calls 'bounce'. 'Logically,' Mr. Forster says,
'*Bleak House* is all to pieces, but Dickens
bounces us, so that we do not mind the shift-
ings of the view-point.' In other words, Mr.
Forster does not mind them: he feels at home
with Dickens and is mistrustful of Henry
James. His attitude, in fact, recalls what
Jules Lemaître once wrote about his own
criticisms: 'Nous avons beau faire (et c'est
là une des infirmités de la critique et une
des raisons qui me font douter si elle est jamais
autre chose que la description et l'analyse
d'impressions toutes personnelles)—nous ne pou-
vons vraiment comprendre et aimer un drame
ou un roman que dans la mesure où nous nous
sentons capables d'éprouver ou, tout au moins,
d'imaginer et de faire nôtres, par la sympathie,
les sentiments des personnages. Il faut que
nous sentions en nous le germe, et un peu
plus que le germe, de ces sentiments.'

Naturally, from what I have said, we find
Henry James's method varying with his choice
of subject. The technique of *The Awkward*

Age is very different from the technique of *The Ambassadors*. But the technique of *What Maisie Knew* closely approaches the technique employed by Mr. de la Mare in *The Almond Tree*. Alter the technique of *Maisie* and you alter the substance. The subject *is* 'what Maisie knew', and therefore nothing her observation would have failed to record can be admitted. That the child's mind is to remain innocent and lovely, and that what we are to see her surrounded by is a narrow world of the vulgarest and most promiscuous uncleanness, may make the task of the novelist enormously difficult, but difficulty never daunted that grand old artist, it acted, on the contrary, as a stimulus. In his first conception of the book he even intended to restrict himself to what his small heroine might be supposed to have understood and interpreted, but experiment showed him his subject 'strangled in that extreme rigour. . . . The infant mind would at the best leave great gaps and voids. . . . I should have to stretch the matter to what my wondering witness materially and inevitably *saw*; a great deal of which quantity she either wouldn't understand at all or would quite misunderstand.

[71]

If the theme had no other beauty it would still have this rare and distinguished one of its so expressing the variety of the child's values . . . she has the wonderful importance of shedding a light far beyond any reach of her comprehension; of lending to poorer passions and things, by the mere fact of their being involved with her and by the special scale she creates for them, a precious element of dignity. . . . The passage in which her father's terms of intercourse with the insinuating but so strange and unattractive lady whom he has had the detestable levity to whisk her off to see late at night, is a signal example of the all but incalculable way in which interest may be constituted. The facts involved are that Beale Farange is ignoble, that the friend to whom he introduces his daughter is deplorable, and that from the commerce of the two, *as* the two merely, we would fain avert our heads. Yet the thing has but to become part of the child's bewilderment for these small sterilities to drop from it and for the *scene* to emerge and prevail—vivid, special, wrought hard, to the hardness of the unforgettable.'

Now it is precisely the poignancy and pathos

springing from his little boy's relation to the actors in a tragedy he can only partially comprehend which Mr. de la Mare beautifully and rightly has seen as the subject of *The Almond Tree*. Nicholas is not on his mother's side, nor on his father's side, nor on the side of Miss Grey. He loves each of them, but he knows—even while he wonders why—that for some reason they cannot all be happy together. Where the author has unnecessarily handicapped himself is in not writing the thing, as Henry James wrote *Maisie*, in the third person. Instead, he makes the Count tell it, as the story of his own childhood. Nothing is gained by this device, and it introduces two dangerous stumbling-blocks which would not otherwise have existed. To begin with, by no stretch of imagination can we see Nicholas growing up to be the Count. The Count is a fantastic silhouette in moonshine, a knight of El Dorado; Nicholas is compact of flesh and blood and passions and intelligence. The only point made by introducing the Count at all, comes at the very end of the story and is entirely immaterial to it. But a greater drawback still is that this eccentric nobleman has to *remember* everything—after forty, fifty years? The story therefore is twice removed from us: we do not get the little boy's impressions directly, but only the Count's memory of them brought out in conversation, and he has to remember too much. 'Bounce', after all then, *does* enter; we must be 'bounced' into credulity if this improbability is to escape our notice.

Let me give an example of what I mean. When the Count (who is Nicholas) remembers how, after his visit to Miss Grey's house, his mother came to him as he lay awake in bed, we believe it, and believe all that he tells us was then spoken between them.

'Where have you been all the evening?' she said.
'Miss Grey asked me to stay to tea,' I answered.
'Did I give you permission to go to tea with Miss Grey?' I made no answer.
'If you go to that house again, I shall beat you. You hear me, Nicholas? Alone, or with your father, if you go there again, without my permission, I shall beat you.'

That he should remember this, I say, is perfectly credible, because it was bound to have produced a deep impression on his mind at the time. But when he remembers and repeats the clever allusive talk of his father, scepticism is aroused.

'Difficult,' he echoed in derision. He checked himself and shrugged his shoulders. 'You see, Jane, it's all on the

[74]

surface; I boast of my indifference. It's the one rag of philosophy age denies no one. It is so easy to be heroic—debonair, iron-grey, fluent, dramatic—you know its captivation, perhaps? But after all, life's comedy, when one stops smiling, is only the tepidest farce. Or the gilt wears off and the pinchbeck tragedy shows through. And so, as I say, we talk on, being past feeling. One by one our hopes come home to roost, our delusions find themselves out, and the mystery proves to be nothing but sleight-of-hand. It's age, my dear Jane—age; it turns one to stone. With you young people life's a dream; ask Nicholas here!' He shrugged his shoulders, adding under his breath, 'But one wakes on a devilish hard pallet.'

That, I feel, the little Nicholas never would have remembered. Such words would have created no impression on his mind, because they could have had very little interest or even meaning for him.

And if we avoid the difficulty by saying that the Count is improvising, what becomes of our *real* little boy? what becomes of that particular element he brought into the story and which was, according to our previous view, so valuable a part of it?

All this may seem hypercritical. Let me hasten to add that if it draws one up for a moment the story none the less remains a thing of delicate and profound beauty, admirably moving and true. The theme is tragic, but

the lamentable things said and done are softened and exquisitely spiritualized by the per-
sonality of the little boy who is the spectator
of their hopeless and inevitable progression,
and who at the same time plays his own small,
half-detached, half-wondering and sympathetic part.   How faithfully he reflects, though
unconscious of their significance, the passions
of the older actors in the drama—his father,
his mother, and the beautiful Miss Grey who
is his friend and yet somehow is the cause of
all their unhappiness! How vividly yet delicately those darker passions of maturity are
contrasted with the innocent selfishness of
childhood—its quaint, superficial callousness
which may at any moment turn to sudden
pity and grief! Of the inner meaning of the
tragedy Nicholas knows little; above all he is
unaware of *one* aspect of it;—how to his mother
it seems to be made yet more wretched, more
wounding and bitter, because soon another
child will be born into that troubled household.

There are passages of an almost intolerable
pathos—the scene of the waiting supper, for
instance—the mother and son waiting, waiting,
waiting for the husband and father who does

not return:—the scene where Nicholas upsets his mother's scent-bottle:

'You foolish, clumsy boy!' said my mother, and slapped my hand. More out of vexation and tiredness than because of the pain, I began to cry. And then, with infinite tenderness, she leaned her head on my shoulder. 'Mother can't think very well just now,' she said; and cried so bitterly in silence that I was only too ready to extricate myself and run away when her hold on me relaxed.

And colour—colour everywhere—the greenness of old gardens, the whiteness of snow, the rich glow of fruit and wine in a candle-lit room, of silver piled on a green card-table, of a deep crimson work-basket by the fire.

Nicholas is among the author's finest studies of childhood. He is strange, wayward, intelligent, infinitely alive, dangerously sensitive, and dangerously impressionable to both good and evil. A chapter, to me of the profoundest interest, might be written on these small heroes of Mr. de la Mare, who strike so individual a note in his work. They are rarely seen in relation to their contemporaries—only once, I think, in *Seaton's Aunt*, and then the relation is a superficial one. They are so convincing and at the same time so unusual that they suggest a single prototype and the collaboration of memory with imagination. In com-

parison, the little girls—of whom Alice in
The Return is perhaps the most beautifully
drawn—seem lured from a remoter world by
spells of love and tenderness. They trail
clouds of glory the boys have lost; they are
the author's darlings, but they are presented
far less intimately. The most unforgettable
perhaps of all these youngsters figures in a
tale which has never been reprinted, but
which was published in *The Monthly Review*
in 1905.

An Ideal Craftsman, to my mind, takes a
high rank among Mr. de la Mare's stories,
not because the writing is without flaw (it is
indeed singularly uneven), but because it is
among the richest in suggestion. Baldly put,
it narrates how a boy during a midnight raid
on a pantry stumbled upon crime and helped
a terrified half-crazed woman to evade the
consequences of murder. Any fairly com-
petent fictionist could make an exciting tale
out of the material used; it is the kind of
thing which treated simply as a sensational
story would tell itself. But that is not Mr. de
la Mare's story. The actual episode, though
appallingly real in its details, as he treats it
becomes only a scarlet pattern on a dense and

mysterious background of life—life looming
up out of the past and stretching on into the
future—life in which, if we pause for a moment,
we can perceive the seeds of other dramas
stirring, swelling, throwing out new tendrils,
coming to dark flower and fruit. There is the
ugly sordid story of the woman's intrigue
with the butler; there is the desolation to which
she goes out as the hall-door slams upon her;
there is the story of a darkened childhood, of
a boyhood turning possibly to evil; the story
of the dead mother; the story of the taciturn
father blind to everything but the new wife's
young beauty; the story of what will follow
when the advent of other children, her own
children, shall have turned in that 'powdery
eyebrowed stepmother' a veiled dislike of the
dead woman's son to active jealousy. And
the actual story we read—of what is it composed? Of a rather disquieting small boy, of
a hidden copy of the Newgate Calendar, of
a body stuffed into a kitchen cupboard, of a
gross and slobbering woman who, driven to
momentary retaliation, has unintentionally committed murder. By what spiritual alchemy
has such material, with its undisguised squalid-
ness, been transformed into beauty? For it

is all beauty, though a sombre and woeful beauty.

'Into secrecy frisked a pampered mouse. A hurried rustling of bed-clothes, the squeak of a dry castor followed, and then the boy sat up on his pillow and set to piecing together reality with not a few scraps of variegated dreams.' The opening sentences are like the rapid lifting of a curtain on a darkened stage: before the end of the paragraph we are roused to expectancy, are somehow listening, listening very intently, to the faint stealthy noises, the creakings and sighings of an old house at night. The note is repeated, and the repetition awakens foreboding, as the boy creeps from his room and comes out on to the dark empty landing. There are rooms to be passed, rooms perhaps less deserted than they seem, rooms whose doors are ajar—like the doors of baited traps.

'Jacobs, he remembered with a qualm' (Jacobs the butler)—'Jacobs had, in a like case, happened upon him at this very spot. He saw in memory the shadow of him now, stepping hastily and oddly in the dusk, white and furious at the sight of the eavesdropper.' Already we know that horror, material as

well as ghostly, is lurking somewhere beyond
the boy's contracted vision, while he hangs
over the dim loop of the staircase. Those
two words 'white' and 'furious' have accom-
plished their purpose: we know that Jacobs,
humming his 'flippant melody through his
teeth', will play a sinister part in whatever is
to happen. 'The man hummed it in content-
ment, superciliously, ironically, in greasy
good humour: he would hum it in his coffin
perhaps.'

Very gradually suspense deepens till it is
scarcely distinguishable from fear. Our nerves
respond with the nerves of this skinny, sallow,
and not particularly innocent adventurer, as, in
his loosely-flapping nightshirt, he descends the
stairs and steals along the narrow draughty
passage, pausing, listening again, hearing now
the pounding of his own heart that is beating
with an ecstasy of mingled excitement and
terror. We are absorbed into his consciousness,
start with his every start, what thrills him thrills
us, what happens in the story really happens,
is tested by all our senses.

This boy is real, the author knows him as
he knows his own mind, and he has given him
his own Scots-French blood. We can see him,

we can hear him, we ourselves are spying, eavesdropping, not reading. He peeps cautiously into the kitchen; he enters, and the woman is there, horribly startled by her unexpected visitor, frightened out of her wits indeed, cajoling, flattering, fawning, sick with fear, her fat face grimacing to a smile as she tries to kiss him, to pet him, to take him on her knee 'in his pretty nightgown'. 'I thought he was his pa; just a little boy; I thought he was his pa'—anything, anything to keep him from questioning, from looking. But those poor muddled wits have little chance against the ice-clear, and ice-*cold* intelligence that takes *her* in at a glance. He does not mind talking to her, humouring the poor fuddled thing, but his dark glinting eyes are not for her, they are attracted by the cupboard door. 'There at the bottom, shut in and swinging with the wind, was a corner of green baize.' Jacobs—the mysteriously absent Jacobs—Jacobs who wears an apron of green baize when he cleans the silver—is in *there*.

He *knows*, knows exactly why Jacobs is hiding so quietly, as if taking a playful part in a game. But the knowledge does not prevent him from opening the door, and as the ugly thing is revealed his first thought is, 'Why, he's quite a little man!'

'How did you do it?' said the boy, taking a cautious step forward. 'Did he struggle? But isn't he tiny?'

The questions were unanswered and unrepeated. That mole upon the bluish clay-coloured cheek was certainly grown blacker.

'You aren't going to leave him like this?' he said sharply. The woman paid him no attention. 'They'd find that out in no time.'

Even in the midst of this callous analysis, the woman's child-like attitude attracted his sympathy. 'Because you know I'd be awfully pleased to help you. I didn't care much for old Jacobs myself. . . . You wouldn't stand the ghost of a chance as it is. They'd catch you easy.'

The woman nodded. 'I don't care; I hope they will. I don't care, 'cause I can't think.'

'That's all rot,' said the boy.

The woman was unpleasing and paradoxical in this mood, and suggestive of a wax model, which, with diabolical tremors, moves its glazed eyes and turns a glossy head. He turned again to the cupboard. . . .

'This would be the first place they would look into,' he said with decision. 'I should look here myself. But don't you see you needn't be caught at all if you do what I tell you. I read it in a book of mine.' The woman lifted a mechanical head and looked at him. She turned and found something perhaps unexpected—a meagre little boy with linnet legs and narrow shoulders, a lean face of bilious brown, with straight brown hair beneath a yachting cap; a boy in stockings and a belt; a boy with narrow dark eyes set steep in his head. She drew on her bonnet and loosened her dress about her throat.

Manifestly she was preparing to go. 'Really, on my honour, it would be all right. A baby could do it.'

[83]

The woman knelt down by his side in a posture not unlike the inmate's of the cupboard. 'Tell me, tell me quick, you silly lamb. What did 'e say—a baby could do it?'

'Yes,' said the boy, outwardly cool, but inwardly ardent, 'it's as easy as A B C. You get a rope and make a noose, and put it over his head and round his neck, you know, just as if he were going to be hanged, and then you hang him up on a nail or something. He mustn't touch the ground, of course. You throttled him, didn't you? You see there's no blood. They'd say he hanged himself, don't you see? They'd find old Jacobs hanging in the kitchen.'

'Oh, I couldn't do it, not for worlds, I couldn't. I'd sooner stop here beside 'im.' She began to sob vacuously.

'You could, I tell you. A baby could do it. . . . I'm going to. . . .'

'I'm not doing it for myself, you know,' he added over his shoulder, as he sallied out to the boot cupboard for a rope.

* * * * *

At last the boy drew back to view his handiwork. This he did with inscrutable face, perhaps a face flattered at his own rare ingenuity, perhaps a face of unsophisticated infamy. Apparently the body swung naturally enough, in some sort resembling the print in his Calendar, yet the consummation was incomplete. One thing was absent, one blemish spoiled the effect, one absent thing robbed it of unity. He stood hunting for it without success.

With sage frowns he followed the woman into the passage. She walked unsteadily, swaying bulkily to and fro, now and again violently colliding with the wall. 'Oh, it was crule, crule,' she was muttering.

After her stalked the boy, deep in thought. When she stopped he stopped; when once more she set forward, as patiently he too set forward with her. . . . This dogged

search after the one thing wanting was in vain. He decided
that it must be looked for in solitude.

'I think you had better go now,' he said. 'He'll be coming
home soon. My father you know——' He saw his
stepmother, hysterical before her swaying manservant. It
faintly, half-sadly tickled his fancy.

All this strikes me as marvellously, absolutely
realized. I know it is true because I can get
inside that boy's mind and test it by experience.
In spite of certain failures (due almost entirely
to a departure from simplicity in the style),
An Ideal Craftsman comes closer to our
ordinary earthly reality than any story Mr.
de la Mare has written except *Missing*, and
the combination of the ugliness of the subject
and the beauty of the spirit and understanding
behind it produces an electrical effect upon
the imagination. I admit that it is very much
my kind of story; by which I mean that
(setting aside the genius that has gone to its
making) it is the kind of story I can easily
picture myself trying to write; but does this
necessarily invalidate one's judgment? And
what a perfect opening chapter for a novel it
would make, simply because we are so interested in its hero and want to know so much
more about him. Perhaps Jimmy, in *Out of
the Deep*, gives us a glimpse of that 'more',

but I think not; I imagine for our Craftsman a life of action, of adventure; I even see hovering above him a shadow of that rope he looped so deftly round the neck of Jacobs. Nicholas, in *The Almond Tree*, is younger brother to him: and Arthur in *Miss Duveen*, and even Tom in *Visitors*, are of his kin. But for me the Craftsman possesses a deeper appeal—an appeal that the very dubiousness of his future strangely intensifies.

Nicholas I dare say is a pleasanter little boy, yet it is not because he is more idealized. We can trust our author in these matters: there will be no attempt made to bring any of these youthful heroes into touch with what the sentimental reader might like them to be, might fancy they *ought* to be. For this, witness Nicholas's discovery of his father's dead body:

I felt no sorrow, but stood beside the body, regarding it only with deep wonder and a kind of earnest curiosity, yet perhaps with a remote pity too, that he could not see me in the beautiful morning. His grey hand lay arched in the snow, his darkened face, on which showed a smear of dried blood, was turned away a little as if out of the oblique sunshine. I understood that he was dead, was already loosely speculating on what changes it would make; how I should spend my time; what would happen in the house now that he was gone, his influence, his authority, his discord. I remembered too that I was alone, was master of this im-

mense secret, that I must go home sedately, as if it were a
Sunday, and in a low voice tell my mother, concealing any
exultation I might feel in the office. I imagined the questions that would be asked me, and was considering the proper
answers to make to them, when my morbid dreams were
suddenly broken in on by Martha Rodd.

That is true, regrettably true perhaps: but
this also is true:

'Look, Martha, look,' I cried, 'I found him in the snow;
he's dead.' And suddenly a bond seemed to snap in my
heart. The beauty and solitude of the morning, the perfect
whiteness of the snow—it was all an uncouth mockery against
me—a subtle and quiet treachery. The tears gushed into
my eyes and in my fear and affliction I clung to the poor girl,
sobbing bitterly, protesting my grief, hiding my eyes in terror
from that still, inscrutable shape.

And again:

My father's body was brought home and laid in my
mother's little parlour that looked out on to the garden and
the snowy orchard. The house was darkened. I took a
secret pleasure in peeping in on the sunless rooms, and stealing
from door to door through corridors screened from the
daylight.

In those early years there are so many
secret pleasures, and these enigmatic heroes
of the de la Mare tales taste of the strangest.
They are exiles from Eden, but they find
their way back for wonderful hours in which
they stand with steadfast eyes undaunted by

the threatening, flaming sword. In all of them, no matter how dark their experience, something of the child survives on into the years of boyhood and manhood. Jimmie, the hero of *Out of the Deep*, is definitely outcast, definitely *not* respectable, yet he is no exception. As for our nameless Craftsman—him I somehow see in close fellowship with that boy spirit, part angel, part devil, who haunted the imagination of Emily Brontë, and became the Heathcliff of *Wuthering Heights* and the Zamorna of her poems. I do not press the point, for the only likeness is in the relation between the creator and his creation, in the emotion behind the conception. Here, at any rate, is one of the Zamorna poems.

> Heavy hangs the rain-drop
>   From the burdened spray;
> Heavy broods the damp mist
>   On uplands far away.
>
> Heavy looms the dull sky,
>   Heavy rolls the sea;
> And heavy throbs the young heart
>   Beneath that lonely tree.
>
> Never has a blue streak
>   Cleft the clouds since morn;
> Never has his grim fate
>   Smiled since he was born.

STORIES REVIVED

Frowning on the infant,
   Shadowing childhood's joy,
Guardian-angel knows not
   That melancholy boy.

Day is passing swiftly
   Its sad and sombre prime;
Boyhood sad is merging
   In sadder manhood's time:

All the flowers are praying
   For sun, before they close,
And he prays too—unconscious—
   That sunless human rose.

Blossom—that the west-wind
   Has never wooed to blow,
Scentless are thy petals,
   Thy dew is cold as snow!

Soul—where kindred kindness
   No early promise woke,
Barren is thy beauty
   As weed upon a rock.

Wither—soul and blossom!
   You both were vainly given:
Earth reserves no blessing
   For the unblest of heaven!

Certain passages in Mr. de la Mare's essay
on *Rupert Brooke and the Intellectual Imagination* seem to fall naturally into place here.

Children, it will be agreed, live in a world peculiarly their

own, so much so that it is doubtful if the adult can do more
than very fleetingly reoccupy that far-away consciousness.
. . . They are not bound in by their groping senses. Facts
to them are the liveliest of chameleons. Between their
dream and their reality looms no impassable abyss. There
is no solitude more secluded than a child's, no absorption
more complete, no insight more exquisite and, one might
even add, more comprehensive. As we strive to look back
and to live our past again, can we recall any joy, fear, hope
or disappointment more extreme than those of our childhood,
any love more impulsive and unquestioning, and, alas, any
boredom so unmitigated and unutterable?

This, even by those who only very rarely
and incompletely have succeeded in reoccupying
'that far-away consciousness', will not be dis-
puted; while for those who have wholly
forgotten the way back, or who find little
interest in retracing it, a part of the work of
our author must ever remain a closed book.

And that callousness of childhood—is it not
after all largely a natural candour and an
enviable freedom from sentimentality?

The child becomes a boy. . . . Apron-strings, however
dear their contents, were always a little restrictive. He
borrows a pitiless pair of scissors. He, unlike the child told
of by Blake and Vaughan and Traherne, had always more
or less 'understood this place'. He loves 'a forward motion'
—the faster the better. When 'shades of the prison-house'
begin to close about him, he immediately sets out to explore
the jail.

Our Craftsman is an expert explorer; the smaller boy in *The Almond Tree* grasps still in one relaxing hand the end of an apron-string; Arthur, in *Miss Duveen*, has dropped the apron-string and is setting out on his first tour of inspection. An amazing discovery he makes: the lady whose name forms the title of this little masterpiece is the first of a series of elderly females nearly as closely allied as their youthful male friends. Miss Duveen, Miss Seaton, Jimmie's Aunt Charlotte, and certain ladies in the poems are members of one family. Of course they differ widely from one another; but so, often, do the actual members of a single family. Miss Duveen's idiosyncrasies are softened by an unfailing amiability: they may, and do eventually, in the rather hard-hearted Arthur, inspire a shamefaced, slightly snobbish distaste, but never fear or hatred. The back of Arthur's garden joined the back of Miss Duveen's garden; a narrow brook flowed between; and across this brook their acquaintance was made, the lady playing the part of wooer, though the gentleman, at this stage of the affair, was by no means unwilling to be wooed.

'Ah,' she said, with a little masculine laugh, 'so this is

the young gentleman, the bold, gallant young gentleman. And what might be his name?'

I replied rather distantly that my name was Arthur.

'Arthur, to be sure!' she repeated with extraordinary geniality, and again, 'Arthur', as if in the strictest confidence.

'I know you, Arthur, very well indeed. I have looked, I have watched; and now, please God, we need never be estranged. . . .'

'Yes, yes, I know you quite intimately, Arthur. We have met *here*.' She tapped her rounded forehead. 'You might not suppose it, too; but I have eyes like a lynx. It is no exaggeration, I assure you—I assure everybody. And now what friends we will be! At times, dear child, I long for company—earthly company.' She glanced furtively about her. 'But I must restrain my longings; and you will, of course, understand that I do not complain. *He* knows best. And my dear cousin, Miss Coppin—she too knows best. She does not consider too much companionship expedient for me. . . .'

Miss Duveen laughed gaily. 'He understands, he understands,' she cried, as if to many listeners. 'Oh, what a joy it is in this world, Arthur, to be understood. Now tell me,' she continued with immense nicety, 'tell me, how's your dear mamma?'

I shook my head.

'Ah,' she cried, 'I see, I see; Arthur has no mamma. We will not refer to it. No father, either?'

I have called *Miss Duveen* a masterpiece, using the word deliberately, to describe a thing that is completely successful and completely individual. No story by any other writer is in the least like it, and no story by Mr. de la

Mare more perfectly does what he intended
it to do. The madness of Miss Duveen floats
through it, gradually changing the aspect of
everything about her from the bizarre to the
painful. For madness is intrinsically shocking,
though this aspect may be hidden, and *is*
hidden in the early stages of Arthur's adventure,
but not towards the end. What Miss Duveen's
life may be when her young friend is not with
her we can only guess: those who look after
her are mere names to us, but there are uncom-
fortable, even dreadful hints of a patience that
is wearing thin—in the end, of neglect, and, possibly, cruelty. Her last appearance is ominous:

I called out loudly I must go in; and still see her gazing
after me, with a puzzled, mournful expression on the face
peering out of the cloak.
Even after that we sometimes waved to one another across
the water, but never if by hiding myself I could evade her
in time. The distance seemed to confuse her, and quite
silenced me. I began to see we were ridiculous friends,
especially as she came now in ever dingier and absurder
clothes. She even looked hungry, and not quite clean, as
well as ill; and she talked more to her phantoms than to me
when once we met.

It is on the whole with distinct relief that
Arthur learns his embarrassing companion has
been put away somewhere out of sight. 'I

should be at ease in the garden again, came the thought—no longer fear to look ridiculous, and grow hot when our neighbour was mentioned, or be saddled with her company beside the stream.'

Poor Miss Duveen!—victim of implacable love—her second lover, it is to be feared, proved no more faithful than her first!

It may be argued that the technique of *Miss Duveen* being similar to that of *The Almond Tree*, the objection I brought against the latter tale should, if valid, hold good here. And it is true both stories are told in the first person and after a long lapse of time; but the fact that in *Miss Duveen* the story is Arthur's *own* story, which happens at the same time to be hers, makes all the difference. Arthur tells us nothing except what he was in a position to understand, appreciate and interpret, therefore his remembering it is no tax to credulity.

Of the remaining tales, with one exception, I must speak more briefly. In the story of *The Bowl* the admirable young Nicholas of *The Almond Tree* reappears, this time unhampered by any compromising relationship with the Count. *The Bowl* is delightful—slight, but very much alive. *The Looking Glass*, on the other hand, seems to me faint, while *The Bird of Travel*, I am afraid, I have somehow missed. I can make out, though dimly, a graceful fancy at the core of it, but nothing sufficiently robust to bear the burden of so much 'treatment'. Where, exactly, *is* the story? All I can recapture is an impression of a bird's song and of a landscape.

There remains *The Riddle*, the briefest of the tales, and in some respects the loveliest. Is it a riddle to which we need seek an answer? Perhaps the title demands that we should; perhaps it is but a warning that we need expect none from the author. For *The Riddle* strikes me as a dream story—a story composed, or experienced, in sleep. The whole thing, I take it, is simply an expression of homesickness, though the reader must discover the identity of that home in his own dreamland. Or forget its challenging title and take it as a fairy story. It is as a fairy story it begins. 'So these seven children, Ann, and Matilda, James, William and Henry, Harriet and Dorothea, came to live with their grandmother.' How beautifully the homely names drop into music. It is the old, familiar, 'once-upon-a-time' beginning, and throughout, the tale is carried on to the same seductive tune. When the little orphans in their black new mourning clothes stand demurely in a row before their granny, the old lady gives to each a present, and to all a warning. They may romp and play to their hearts' content in every room in the house; only in the large spare bedroom that looks out on the slate roof there stands in the corner an old oak chest. 'Play anywhere else in the house,' their grandmother tells them kindly, 'but not there.'

It is the Blue Beard motif, but it is anything but a Blue Beard story. It is the story of an allurement soft as sleep. A voice whispers from far away—whispers one word, 'Come'— and at the sound all power of resistance melts like snow.

It was evening twilight when Henry went upstairs from the nursery by himself to look at the oak chest. He pressed his fingers into the carved fruit and flowers, and spoke to the dark-smiling heads at the corners; and then, with a glance over his shoulder, he opened the lid and looked in. But the chest concealed no treasure, neither gold nor baubles, nor was there anything to alarm the eye. The chest was empty, except that it was lined with silk of old-rose, seeming darker in the dusk, and smelling sweet of pot-pourri. And while Henry was looking in, he heard the softened laughter and the clinking of the cups downstairs in the nursery; and out at the window he saw the day darkening. These things brought strangely to his memory his mother who in her glimmering white dress used to read to him in the dusk; and he climbed into the chest; and the lid closed gently down over him.

The Riddle is not a ghost story, nor does fear even remotely enter into it. The dreamy caressing magic which draws the children one by one into the old, silk-lined, faintly fragrant chest, till at last the grandmother is left alone in the great solitary house, works through beauty. Beauty—and perhaps through love—and above all through homesickness, for what else does it whisper of to Henry but the home where his mother stands waiting for him on the threshold? The dark-smiling heads Henry touches with his fingers are very dear to Mr. de la Mare: they will appear again more than once in his work, always with the deep fascination of their silent mystery. In *The Return* Arthur Lawford sees them carved in ruined stone over the lintel of Death's Door. But beyond that door for Lawford is only an utter darkness: here it leads back to the golden shore of childhood, to a region where the lost days are gathered, the lost playmates found, the lost love fulfilled.

The effect of the rich emotional content of the story becomes, as nearly always with Mr. de la Mare, immediately visible in the simplicity

G

of the writing. But the mood of reverie from which the thing has sprung is not quite the reverie of childhood. There is a hint of world-weariness in it for all its tenderness. In this mood the poet is half in love with death, wholly in love with death's garden. Such a mood haunts a good many pages of *The Return*, and every page of *Ding Dong Bell*, that strange little book which is neither wholly essay nor wholly story, and which I am inclined to bring in here, for though it was not published till 1924 it is nevertheless a comparatively early thing revised. Quaint, whimsical, and delightful, it is. The author loiters among the crumbling head-stones in a country church-yard, loiters among graves, worms, and epitaphs, and all the epitaphs are written by himself. A faintly macabre note is struck once or twice, but for the most part a playful friendliness prevails, an affection tinged with humour.

> No Voice to scold;
>   No face to frown;
> No hand to smite
>   The helpless down:
> Ay, Stranger, here
>   An Infant lies,
> With worms for
>   Welcome Paradise.

The three chapters into which the book is divided have titles that are like the titles of Mr. de la Mare's lyrics: *Lichen*, '*Benighted*', *Winter*. The happy jumble of prose and verse in itself suggests the over-grown, tree-shaded paths, the mossy crumbling tombstones, the luxuriant grasses and sweet-scented brambles of an ancient and not too carefully-tended graveyard. Dark pools of shadow cast by cypress and yew contrast with the flaming scarlet of a flowering-currant: birds have dropped seeds which have taken root between ever-widening crannies; and in that corner 'where the birds come to drink, is the figure of a boy, standing there, in cold stone, listening. How many times, I wonder, have I scurried like a rabbit at twilight past his shrine. And yet, no bones there; only a passing reminder':

> Finger on lip I ever stand;
>   Ay, stranger, quiet be;
> This air is dim with whispering shades
>   Stooping to speak to thee.

But the stooping shades do not speak to tell their secret: *that* is still guarded: the riddle is unanswered.

[99]

WALTER DE LA MARE

'Is that John Simpson?'
'Ay, it be.'
'What was thy age, John?'
'Eighty-three.'
'Wast happy in life, John?'
'Life is vain.'
'What then of death, friend?'
'Ask again.'

CHAPTER VI

POEMS (1906)

I INTEND this to be a short chapter, for, though we return in it to the verse, it will be a great deal more profitable to linger over the later poems than over those published in 1906. Much of this second book of verse is transitional. In the intellectual and objective poetry it contains, Mr. de la Mare is breaking new ground, but it is significant that while only six of the *Songs of Childhood* were omitted from the Collected Edition of his poems, sixteen of these later pieces were rejected: *Juliet, Desdemona, Casca, 'Come!', The Winter Boy, Ev'n Rosemary, Coup de Grâce, Messengers, Irrevocable, Winter Coming, Omniscience, Youth, The Voice of Melancholy, Portrait of a Boy, Unpausing,* and *The Seas of England*.

Looking back at it to-day, the little book seems, in fact, to stand rather oddly apart from the author's other works. Only here and there has it anything in common with *Songs of Child-hood*, yet can we truly say that it foreshadows either *The Listeners* or *Peacock Pie*? One might almost hazard the view that certain elements in it, after having lain fallow for many years, passed, deepened and transformed, into the poetry of *The Veil*.

I remember when I read it first—still dazzled as I was by *Songs of Childhood*—I found it disappointing. This was a stupid view; but things like *Goliath*, *Youth*, the thirteen *Characters from Shakespeare*, struck me then, and for that matter still strike me, as being hardly poems. They are amazingly 'wrought', their brilliant blank verse is closely packed with metaphor—packed indeed to the point of obscurity—but each line is made to carry too heavy a burden, and no line recaptures the natural note of speech. Even in the sonnets, fine as they are, the poet seems to be working against the true inclination of his genius, which is, we now begin to suspect, exclusively lyrical.

It was these extraneous, these didactic and descriptive pieces, comprising as they did more than half the volume, that prevented me in the old days from doing it justice. Stupidity, I repeat: because in the lyrics themselves the

magic reawakens, and it is a deeper magic than
the early märchen glamour:

'Who called?' I said, and the words
   Through the whispering glades,
Hither, thither, baffled the birds—
   'Who called?   Who called?'

The leafy boughs on high
   Hissed in the sun;
The dark air carried my cry
   Faintingly on:

Eyes in the green, in the shade,
   In the motionless brake,
Voices that said what I said,
   For mockery's sake:

'Who cares?' I bawled through my tears:
   The wind fell low:
In the silence, 'Who cares? who cares?'
   Wailed to and fro.

And this:

Green Mistletoe!
Oh, I remember now
A dell of snow,
Frost on the bough;
None there but I:
Snow, snow, and a wintry sky.

[103]

None there but I,
And footprints one by one,
Zigzaggedly,
Where I had run;
Where shrill and powdery
A robin sat in the tree.

And he whistled sweet;
And I in the crusted snow
With snow-clubbed feet.
Jigged to and fro,
Till, from the day,
The rose-light ebbed away.

And the robin flew
Into the air, the air,
The white mist through;
And small and rare
The night-frost fell
Into the calm and misty dell.

And the dusk gathered low,
And the silver moon and stars
On the frozen snow
Drew taper bars,
Kindled winking fires
In the hooded briars.

And the sprawling Bear
Growled deep in the sky;
And Orion's hair
Streamed sparkling by:
But the North sighed low,
'Snow, snow, more snow!'

POEMS

Such poems are even more really songs of childhood than the *Songs* themselves were. As immediately, and far more profoundly, they pierce into the heart and brain. They are lovelier and sadder than the early songs. The atmosphere is utterly different. There are no more fairies and witches, wolves and dwarfs and ogres: all that jolly company is gone. There is less excitement and more uneasiness. Houses, woods, and rivers are still haunted— only the haunters now are invisible. It is this uncertainty that is disquieting. There is a perpetual question and no answer. It is the first sounding of that note which is repeated with a deeper and darker significance in *The Veil*, where it turns at times almost to despair.

> What voice is that I hear
> Crying across the pool?

No voice such as summoned Sleepyhead to his window, but a voice that lures 'to darkness deep and black'.

> Comes no more dawn to me,
>   Nor bird of open skies.
> Only his woods' deep gloom I see
>   Till, at the end of all, shall rise,
> Afar and tranquilly,
> Death's stretching sea.

Yet there are kinder voices, too: there always will be: though the speakers remain hidden.

> Who is it calling by the darkened river
> Where the moss lies smooth and deep,
> And the dark trees lean unmoving arms,
> Silent and vague in sleep,
> And the bright-heeled constellations pass
> In splendour through the gloom;
> Who is it calling o'er the darkened river
> In music, 'Come!'?
>
> .   .   .   .
>
> Who is it watching in the gathering twilight,
> When the curfew bird hath flown
> On eager wings, from song to silence,
> To its darkened nest alone?
> Who takes for brightening eyes the stars,
> For locks the still moonbeam,
> Sighs through the dews of evening peacefully—
> Falling, 'Dream!'?

Dream—yes: 'the lost traveller's dream under the hill'. In these lyrics Mr. de la Mare's genius is undergoing an inevitable transformation, for, sooner or later, songs of innocence must pass into songs of experience. With his widening and deepening view of life has come a momentary hesitation: hence so many unaccustomed paths struck out and followed for a short distance before finally they are abandoned. And though we know they were wisely abandoned, we cannot but feel that they too served a purpose, if no other than that of making plain to him his way.

CHAPTER VII

THE THREE MULLA-MULGARS (1910)

INNUMERABLE are the story books that have been written for children, but (setting aside a few collections of folk and fairy tales) it was not till well on in the last century, I should say, that in children's authors the spirit of the Shorter Catechism began to yield to a desire to give pleasure. The desire straightway produced a masterpiece, *Alice's Adventures in Wonderland*. That was more than half a century ago, but in nursery literature *Alice* has never been surpassed—never, for that matter, equalled, except by Lewis Carroll's second tale, *Through the Looking-Glass*.

What, then, is the secret of these books' perennial charm? It lies, I think, not only in their humour and originality, in the extraordinary power of invention that has created incident after incident and yet contrived to keep all related in a perfect dream sequence, but also in their possession of two further virtues, lacking which they could not have attained and kept their unique position. The first of these virtues is that they are *pitched* exactly right: except for *Jabberwocky* (a brilliant misjudgment, but nevertheless a misjudgment so far as the child is concerned), I doubt if we get anything from them at the age of twenty-four or forty-eight that we did not get at twelve. The second is that they have the air of improvisations: the *Alices* obviously are being *told* to their audience, and we know the persuasiveness of the spoken word.

One Sunday morning, a good many years ago, I came upon an odd little gathering in a public park. The park was situated in the Roman Catholic quarter of my native town, and the gathering was composed of about a dozen persons of both sexes, whose ages, at a guess, averaged between seven and ten. Both the hour and the place indicated that the members of this interesting group belonged to the elder faith, and the centre of it was a remarkably bright-eyed but far from lovely little girl, a year or two older than the rest. They all belonged to the poorest class; they all were ragged, untidy, and more or less unwashed; they all were spell-bound, though the spell was

broken every now and again by a general burst
of laughter to which even the smallest con-
tributed; and they all were listening to the
bright-eyed child who, after one swift smile at
the intruder, continued to read aloud from a
torn and grimy copy of *Alice in Wonderland*.

That scene, I don't know why, has remained
a vivid memory; producing, moreover, when-
ever I think of it, the surprising effect of turning
me into a potential socialist. *Alice* was written
for nice little girls of the Sixties, who sat
docilely on the knees (cultured but uncomfort-
able) of elderly Oxford dons. The first copy
was presented to Miss Alice Liddell, but the
second, I am afraid, went to the Princess
Beatrice. Here, however—under this alien
sky, amid this far from distinguished company
—were the Duchess and the Cook and the
Baby, the Cheshire Cat and the Frog Footman,
all merry as grigs and perfectly at home. Jokes
were greeted with peals of laughter, and *no*
joke was missed. It was an odd picture,
singularly pleasing, yet, if one happened to
be sentimentally inclined, singularly pathetic.
The reader's accent was deplorable, her habit
of suddenly pausing and reading on rapidly and
silently ahead before returning to her impatient

audience, was trying, but the genius which had created that fantastic dream tale for all time and for every child emerged triumphantly from the ordeal.

Now can we apply the touchstone of *Alice* to Mr. de la Mare's *Three Mulla-Mulgars*? I think not. At any rate, all we shall learn by doing so is that the books must be placed on different shelves. Is Mr. de la Mare's book, then, not for the nursery? That, again, is a matter for each nursery to decide. I should think it unlikely that it is for the rather forlorn one I have depicted here: it is pitched, I am afraid, above *those* not very clean, and yet somehow strangely lovable heads: and it is, most emphatically, *written*. The prose of Lewis Carroll is plain and homely as the prose of Ma Mère l'Oye, as the prose, indeed, of any gifted old nurse, who with one eye on the clock and the other on her small band of listeners, turns 'the firelight hours to a dream of gold': but much of the enchantment of Mr. de la Mare's tale is produced by the beauty of the writing. True, any intelligent child will enjoy the adventures; but only a rather rare little mortal will grasp all the older reader grasps.

I must admit that I myself quite fail to grasp

what an enthusiastic critic, Mr. R. L. Mégroz, refers to when he talks of the 'profundity of the satire behind the fairy tale'. 'When we first have our eyes fully opened to this is when Nod, lost and parted awhile from his distressed brothers, falls into the hands of an "Oomgar", or man.' Now, it seems to me that at even the faintest breath of satire every flower and leaf in this particular garden would wilt and wither. The satirical is not Mr. de la Mare's province; it is foreign to the whole temper of his mind. There is irony in *The Midget* and in certain chapters of *The Return*; and there is humour in both books, in *The Mulla-Mulgars*, and in many of the poems; but of satire, I venture to say, not a hint.

The Three Mulla-Mulgars, now called *The Three Royal Monkeys*, was written for, and read aloud to the author's own children. On its publication it met with scant success, and it took many years to sell out the first edition. One cannot help feeling how large an element of chance there is in these things. Some books get known immediately, while others, for no discoverable reason, never get known at all outside an appreciative but slender circle of readers. They are like the shy children at parties, who remain hovering in the background—in corners, behind palms, even behind the piano—while their noisier and bolder, not to say brazen, comrades are attracting all the attention. For there can be no doubt that, taking it merely as a story, *The Mulla-Mulgars* is among the most amusing and exciting ever offered to intelligent boys and girls. Its strangeness is no handicap so far as they are concerned: what may have proved a handicap, what certainly could not have *helped* it, is the number of difficult and invented words in the opening chapter. It is unfortunate that these words should be scattered so much more thickly over the first pages than over the rest of the book. The less persevering young reader may very well be discouraged by 'Exxzwixxia', 'Azmamogreel', 'Oggewibbies', 'Garniereze': how can he tell he has only to break through this somewhat prickly hedge to find himself in the most thrilling and variegated world of wonder and adventure!

But not in fairyland: the book is not in the ordinary sense a fairy tale, though there is magic in it, and Nod, the hero, is the youngest of three brothers. The brothers are monkeys, princes born in exile, and the story tells of their perilous journey in search of their Uncle Assasimmon's kingdom, which lies far away in the beautiful Valleys of Tishnar, 'beyond and beyond, forest and river, forest swamp and river, the mountains of Arakkaboa, leagues, leagues away.' Thumma, Thimbulla, Ummanodda—Thumb, Thimble, and Nod—are their names. They can talk; all the animals in the book can talk; and this gift of speech brings them very close to humans. Does it bring them too close for reality? The question would only be pertinent if the story were a realistic animal story, which it isn't; and Thumb, Thimble, and Nod are alive and convincing. A love of beasts fills the book. We had a glimpse of it in *Henry Brocken*, in the portrait of Rosinante, and we get further glimpses in the poems—a thing like *Nicholas Nye*, for instance, could only be written by an animal lover. Mr. de la Mare writes of animals as he writes of children: Henry and Nicholas are addressed in just the same tone of half-bantering affection.

> Thick in its glass
>   The physic stands,
> Poor Henry lifts
>   Distracted hands;

His round cheek wans
   In the candlelight,
To smell that smell!
   To see that sight!

Finger and thumb
   Clinch his small nose,
A gurgle, a gasp,
   And down it goes;
Scowls Henry now;
   But mark that cheek,
Sleek with the bloom
   Of health next week!

Nicholas Nye was lean and grey,
   Lame of a leg and old,
More than a score of donkey's years
   He had seen since he was foaled;
He munched the thistles, purple and spiked,
   Would sometimes stoop and sigh,
And turn to his head, as if he said,
      'Poor Nicholas Nye!'

      .   .   .   .

Seem to be smiling at me, he would,
   From his bush in the corner, of may——
Bony and ownerless, widowed and worn,
   Knobble-kneed, lonely and grey;
And over the grass would seem to pass
   'Neath the deep dark blue of the sky,
Something much better than words between me
      And Nicholas Nye.

But dusk would come in the apple boughs,
   The green of the glow-worm shine,

The birds in nest would crouch to rest,
　　And home I'd trudge to mine;
And there, in the moonlight, dark with dew,
　　Asking not wherefore nor why,
Would brood like a ghost, and as still as a post,
　　Old Nicholas Nye.

Both Henry and Nicholas clearly are inmates of the poet's world: no need for unbending or condescending: all three could pass a contented afternoon together, though each might be busy with his own thoughts.

What is so refreshing about *The Mulla-Mulgars* is this natural understanding. The monkeys' thoughts, we feel, even when they are very like our own rather better thoughts, are still monkey thoughts. Nod is perhaps more than three-quarters way between beast and human; the difference between him and a pleasant but unusually grave little boy is slight; still it is there and is maintained consistently. He is an exceptional monkey of course, a small super-monkey, not only a prince but a Nizza-neela, which means a pet, one dear to the gods and specially guarded by them: in the Bible the infant Samuel is a Nizza-neela. Nod's brothers Thumb and Thimble—in whom the beast is much more strongly marked—bully

him a little, but they are very fond of him.
And he has the Wonderstone his mother gave
him before she died.   This Wonderstone really
is the gift of Tishnar, who is the spirit of good,
of life and love; just as Immanâla is the spirit
of evil and fear and death.   When Nod spits
on his Wonderstone and rubs it, Tishnar helps
him: without his Wonderstone the brothers
would never have come safely through the
dangers and pitfalls of their wild journey, and
it is with the help of his Wonderstone he saves
the life of Andy Battle, the shipwrecked sailor
and the only human in the novel.   The adventure of his meeting with Battle and of their
friendship is the beautiful centre of the book.
So finely conceived and written is it, so true
to both man and beast, that we reluctantly
accept it as but an episode in this odyssey, and
watch Nod making his preparations for departure.   There are dangers of every kind, natural
and supernatural; there are enemies strong and
crafty and very hungry; the track itself at times
is nearly impassable, and that winter of con-
tinuous ice and frost and snow is maybe the
greatest danger of all.

It is strange that this radiant, iridescent,
winter beauty should haunt a tale of the tro-

pics; but its dazzling whiteness of moon-fire
and glittering frost gives the entire book a
colour scheme definite as that of an actual
picture, and diametrically opposed to the no
less definite colour scheme of *The Return*.
The air, too, is thinner, colder, more bracing
than the air we breathe in *The Return*: it is
difficult to explain how it is created, but the
effect none the less sharply impresses itself
upon us that the whole thing is written an
octave higher. A mysterious music sounds
through it, always high up in the treble clef
—clear, insistent, unearthly—a music of strings
and harps. It is a story of copious incident
and adventure, but it is kept from first to
last on the plane of poetry. The element of
wonder in it is not the irresponsible wonder-
working of the old nursery tales; it is more
imaginative, more real. There is a vast difference between the wicked troll of Asbjörnsen
or Grimm and Mr. de la Mare's Immanâla.
This dire creation, half ghostly, half reptilian,
as she writhes in her tight cloak—tall, slender,
undulating, with her grey flattened head, her
long neck, her colourless glassy eyes, her faint
gigglings and whimperings—is the very incar-
nation of fear, cruelty, and treachery. Simi-

larly Tishnar, bright starry spirit of the hills
—pure, shining, yet softened with compassion
—bears no resemblance to any queen of fairyland. She is not a creation of fancy; she is
the divine protectress, the spiritual guardian,
the mother goddess. She is at once the
universal mother and all 'that which cannot
be thought about in words, or told, or expressed'. She is the 'secret and quiet world
beyond the Mulgars' lives . . . wind and stars,
too, the sea and the endless unknown. . . .
She is shown veiled on the rude pots of Assasimmon and in Mulgar scratch-work, with one
slim-fingered hand clasping her robe of palest
purple, her head bent a little, as if hearkening
to her thoughts.' We see her in this description as sister to the lady Hekate, daughter of
Persaeus, in the beautiful hymn to Demeter,
'sitting in her cave, half veiled with a shining
veil, thinking delicate thoughts'. But only
outwardly does she resemble the Greek goddess,
for Tishnar is the goddess not of midnight fears
and spectres but of poetry, of the kind of poetry,
above all, we find in this book.

Twice in the course of the journey Nod
loses his Wonderstone, and twice he regains it.
The first time it is after a fight with eagles,

high up on a narrow mountain pass, and he has no hope of finding it, for it must have fallen into the abyss.

He sat there with chattering teeth, his little skull crouching in his wool, worn out with travel and sleeplessness, and the tears sprang scalding into his eyes. What would Thumb say now? he thought bitterly. What hope was left for Thimble? He dared not wake them, but stooped there like a little bowed old man, utterly forlorn. And so sitting, cunning Sleep, out of the silence and darkness of Arakkaboa, came softly hovering above the troubled Nizza-neela; he fell into a shallow slumber. And in this witching slumber he dreamed a dream.

He dreamed it was time gone by, and that he was sitting on his log again with his master, Battle, just as they used to sit, beside their fire. And the Oomgar had a great flat book covering his knees. Nod could see the book marvellously clearly in his dream—a big book, white as a dried palm-leaf, that stretched across the sailor knee to knee. And the sailor was holding a little stick in his hand, and teaching him, as he used in a kind of sport to do, his own strange 'Ningllish' tongue. Before, however, the sailor had taught the little Mulgar only in words, by sound, never in letters, by sight. But now in Nod's dream Battle was pointing with his little prong, and the Mulgar saw a big straddle-legged black thing in the book strutting all across the page.

'Now,' said the Oomgar, and his voice sounded small but clear, 'what's that, my son?'

But Nod in his dream shook his head; he had never seen the strange shape before.

'Why, that's old "A", that is,' said Battle; 'and what did old straddle-legs "A" go for to do? What did "A" do, Nod Mulgar?'

And Nod thought a voice answered out of his own mouth and said: ' "A" . . . Yapple-pie.'

'Brayvo!' cried the Oomgar. And there, sure enough, filling plump the dog's-eared page, was a great dish something like a gourd cut in half, with smoke floating up from a little hole in the middle.

' "A"—Apple-pie,' repeated the sailor; 'and I wish we had him here, Master Pongo. And now, what's this here?' He turned the page.

Nod seemed in his dream to stand and to stare at the odd double-bellied shape, with its long straight back, but in vain. 'Bless ye, Nod Mulgar,' said Battle in his dream, 'that's old Buzz-buzz; that's that old garden-robber—that's "B".'

' "B",' squealed Nod.

'And "B"—he bit it,' said Battle, clashing his small white teeth together and laughing, as he turned the page.

Next in the dream-book came a curled black fish, sitting looped up on its tail. And that, the Oomgar told him, leaning forward in the firelight, was 'C'; that was 'C'—crying, clawing, clutching, and croaking for it.

Nod thought in his dream that he loved learning, and loved Battle teaching him, but that at the word 'croaking' he looked up wondering into the sailor's face, with a kind of waking stir in his mind. What was this 'IT'? What could this 'IT' be—hidden in the puffed-out, smoking pie that 'B' bit, and 'C' cried for, and swollen 'D' dashed after? And . . . over went another crackling page. . . . The Oomgar's face seemed strangely hairy in Nod's dream; no, not hairy—tufty, feathery; and so loud and shrill he screamed 'E', Nod all but woke up.

' "E",' squeaked Nod timidly after him.

'And what—what—what did "E" do?' screamed the Oomgar.

But now even in his dream Nod knew it was not the

beloved face of his sailor Zbaffle, but an angry, keen-beaked, clamouring, swooping Eagle that was asking him the question, ' "E", "E", "E"—what did "E" do?' And clipped in the corner of its beak dangled a thread, a shred of his sheep's jacket. What ever, ever did 'E' do? puzzled in vain poor Nod, with that dreadful face glinting almost in touch with his.

'Dunce! Dunce!' squalled the bird. ' "E" ate it. . . ,'

' "E" . . . ate it,' seemed to be faintly echoing on his ear in the darkness when Nod found himself wide awake and bolt upright, his face cold and matted with sweat, yet with a heat and eagerness in his heart he had never known before. He scrambled up and crept along in the rosy firelight till he came to the five dead eagles. Their carcasses lay there with frosty feathers and fast-sealed eyes. From one to another he crept slowly, scarcely able to breathe, and turned the carcasses over. Over the last he stooped, and—a flock, a thread of sheep's wool dangled from its clenched black beak. Nod dragged it, stiff and frozen, nearer the fire, and with his knife slit open the deep-black, shimmering neck, and there, wrapped damp and dingily in its scrap of Oomgar paper, his fingers clutched the Wonderstone.

The second time, he lends it to a Water Midden, who swims away with it. But the Midden is tender-hearted, and only for a few anxious hours keeps his treasure from him. Beautiful is this scene of childish love, but it is too long to quote and abridgment would spoil it. Let me give instead a landscape, a glimpse of Tishnar's orchards, where, near their journey's end, a feast of strange fruits awaits the travellers—strange to them, but familiar to us, though not one is named by its name.

So at last it was agreed between them. And Thumb and Nod returned together to the edge of the wood and peered out once more towards the phantom-guarded orchards. Nod waited no longer. He wetted his thumb once more, and rubbed thrice, droning or crooning, and stamping nimbly in the snow, till suddenly Thumb sprang clean into the midst of a thorn-tree in his dismay.

For the child stood there in the snow, shining as if his fur were on fire with silver light. About his head a wreath of moon-coloured buds like frost-flowers was set. His shoulders were hung with a robe like spider-silk falling behind him to his glistening heels. But it was Nod's shrill small laughter that came out of the shining. . . .

Thumb grunted, beat once on his chest like a Gunga, and they stepped boldly out together, first Nod, then black Thumb, into the wide splendour of the waste. . . . Out into the open snow that borders for leagues the trees of Tishnar's orchard stepped Nod, with his Wonderstone. And, as he moved along, the frost-parched flakes burned with the rainbow. . . . Nod's light heels fell so fast Thumb could scarcely keep pace with him. He came on grunting and coughing, plying his thick cudgel, his great dark eyes fixed stubbornly upon the snow. And lo and behold! when Nod next lifted his face he saw only moonlight shining upon the smooth trunks of trees, which in the higher branches were stooping with coloured fruit. He laughed aloud. 'See, Thumb,' he said, 'my magic burns. These are nought but trees!'

But Thumb stared in more dismal terror still, for he saw plainly now their huge and shadowy clubs, their necklets

of gold and ivory, and the hideous, purple-capped faces of the
ghouls gloating down on him.

The adventures at this stage are almost over.
The travellers are not within sight of it indeed,
but they are very near their Happy Valley.
They reach it in the end by taking a last
desperate risk. Down the black smooth sub-
terranean river, whose current sucks their raft
under the impassable Arakkaboa Mountains,
they float—as Alan Quatermain once floated
—at a terrific speed, and through an unknown
and awful darkness, out into the quiet sunlight
of Assasimmon's Kingdom.

The book breaks off somewhat abruptly, but
with the half-promise of a sequel—a sequel
which will never now be written. It never,
I think, could have been written; for our
travellers are home, and that is the end. A
description of their home would be an anti-
climax, and would moreover deprive the reader
of the pleasure of imagining it for himself.
And all through, the book is written so that
he can if he likes view in it his own earthly
pilgrimage. I do not mean that there is the
least suggestion of allegory: I do not believe
the author had any other thought than of his
monkeys' adventures while he was writing it.

Still, its beauty relates it to the main body of
Mr. de la Mare's work: behind earth's loveliness hovers a dream of the absolute: a divine
discontent awakens in it and is comforted.

CHAPTER VIII

THE RETURN (1910)

IN Henry James's *Embarrassments* there is a tale, *The Next Time*, which fancifully perhaps, but by now permanently, is associated in my mind with *The Return*. The reader may remember the story. It is one of a group, first-fruits of that marvellous 'second manner', in which the master is trying his wings, so to speak, before launching out on the sustained flight of a full-length novel. The subjects of these unique and beautiful experiments—*The Figure in the Carpet*, *The Middle Years*, *The Death of the Lion*, *The Coxon Fund*—are as a rule literary subjects, though the most beautiful of all, *The Altar of the Dead*, has nothing to do with literature. But *The Next Time* is a literary story, it is simply the history of Ray Limbert's bid for popularity, his efforts to 'wake up the libraries'—efforts defeated each time by his own genius, 'the purity of the gift'.

The relation of Ray Limbert's undertaking

to *The Return*, however, requires a closer
explanation than this, and, if I am to furnish
one, I must go back to a summer afternoon
many years ago, to an upper room in the St.
George's Café, and to a talk that had not begun
as, but had presently drifted into, a search for
those qualities one might imagine as conducive
to success in literature.   Success in its real sense,
of course, had been defined by James himself:
—a man had achieved it 'when of a beautiful
subject his expression was complete': it was
'success in the line of one's idiosyncrasy'; 'consistency was in itself distinction'.   And James's
own later novels were a beautiful example of it,
even the extremely faint encouragement they
had received from the ordinary novel-reading
public being turned by enthusiasm into a
tribute to their art.   It was not a very satis-
factory tribute—the wildest enthusiasm could
scarcely see it as that—but it was somehow
endearing, appealing.   After all, though one
might express indignation at its failure to do
so, did one really *want The Spoils of Poynton*
to make a big spectacular splash in the promiscuous pond of fiction?   Did one not
secretly, and perhaps selfishly, cherish it all the
more just because it left those viscid waters so

untroubled? Its lovers were members of a community, if not religious very nearly so: they had the comforting and rather rare surety that everybody who cared for the thing understood it, cared for its delicacy and beauty: since it wasn't disgraceful *not* to admire it, admiration, where it did occur, was the more likely to be genuine.

But it was around success in a much vulgarer sense—success as understood by the libraries and book-shops—success as represented by 'sales'—that the conversation I refer to hovered: and presently there emerged the startling confidence that *The Return* was a bid for it, had been designed deliberately as a sensational story, a 'shocker', a thing the public would infallibly rise to, would recognize as its own. So Henry James's story was true!—or had come true after fourteen years!—and as if to add a further verisimilitude one of the interlocutors found himself precisely in the position of the narrator of the tale.[1] 'Coming home to dinner I found the volume on my table, and I sat up with it half the night, dazed, bewildered, rubbing my eyes. . . . Obvious?—where the deuce was it

[1] I have an uneasy suspicion that he has also dropped into his manner—the most contagious of any I know.

obvious? Popular?—how on earth could it be popular? The thing was charming with all his charm and powerful with all his power: it was an unscrupulous, an unsparing, a shameless, merciless masterpiece. . . . It is grimly droll to reflect that this superb little composition, the shortest of his novels, but perhaps the loveliest, was planned from the first as an "adventure-story" on approved lines. It was the way they all did the adventure-story that he tried most dauntlessly to emulate. I wonder how many readers ever divined to which of their bookshelves *The Hidden Heart* was so exclusively addressed. . . . As soon as I read the deep and delicate thing I knew, as I had known in each case before, exactly how well it would do.'

Looking back at it to-day, I find nothing to add to this. *The Return* certainly is the most broadly human and the most simply written of the de la Mare romances: it is likewise the most intimate. But its very intimacy is incompatible with popularity: its appeal is *not* universal; it is *not* addressed to the masses; it does *not* contain general ideas or an approved point of view. It has been called fantastic, but it is not fantastic: it has been called morbid,

but in what truly is morbid there lurks always
the trail of an obsession, of something from
which the author is powerless to escape, which
he may thrust out of sight but which perpetually comes back again, sounding through
his work like the obstinate buzzing of a fly;
and I need hardly say that there is nothing in
the least resembling this in *The Return*. On
the contrary, imagination in it soars and circles
in a clear air of complete intellectual and
spiritual freedom.

The book won for its author the de Polignac
Prize; nevertheless, like *Songs of Childhood*, like
Henry Brocken, like *The Three Mulla-Mulgars*,
it failed to reach the general public. A con-
temporary review of it pointed out how much
more admirably the subject would have been
treated by Mr. H. G. Wells; and this pro-
nouncement, too striking readily to be forgotten, may lead us to ask what the subject
actually is. We certainly shall not find an
answer in anything that happens *to* Lawford
(whose story it is), but only in what happens
within him. As I see it, in fact, the subject is
not unakin to that of Wordsworth's famous
Ode; only the action is reversed. I mean that,
from the shades of his prison-house Lawford

moves gradually back, following through storm, gloom, and danger a 'visionary gleam' which *may* be the light of home.

I have said the book is not fantastic, and I would add that its strength lies in its reality. We never for a moment get out of reality; always we feel its firm ground under our feet. An appalling accident happens to Lawford at the beginning of the tale, but there are no more accidents.   It is the story of a spiritual upheaval such as might be produced by any violent emotional crisis, religious or otherwise.   The actual cause, in comparison with its con-sequences, is unimportant.   Mr. de la Mare characteristically seeks it outside the range of normal experience—on the rim, as it were, of the necromancer's circle, beyond which hover shapes of a supernatural dreadfulness and beauty.   Thus he gets his strangeness, his atmosphere, the peculiar *kind* of beauty that most appeals to him.

The novel, however, is to be a novel of real life.   Therefore, if it is to have this strangeness and beauty, it must be presented to us through an intelligence deeply sensitive to these quali-ties.   The small, though extremely capable and practical mind of Sheila, for example, would

not do. No light from the other kingdom
could ever be reflected in *that* mirror without
immediately losing its significance, without
having all its values altered and cheapened.
Actually we get the story entirely through
Lawford himself: that is to say, he is the only
character whom the author 'goes behind'. It
is obvious then that the real Lawford cannot
be the Lawford Sheila and her friends know
—the dull, commonplace, successful business-
man; the middle-aged, lethargic, heavily con-
scientious husband, father, and neighbour
whom we ourselves, as he first crosses the
threshold of our vision, might almost take him
to be, were it not for a gleam of warning light
momentarily cast back upon a boyhood subject
to 'fits of a kind of fishlike day-dream'. 'How
often, and even far beyond boyhood, had he
found himself bent on some distant thought
or fleeting vision that the sudden clash of self-
possession had made to seem quite illusory, and
yet had left so strangely haunting. And now
the old habit had stirred out of its long sleep,
and, through the gate that Influenza in depart-
ing had left ajar, had returned upon him.'
    None the less, it is a very jaded and apathetic
Lawford in whom these listless thoughts arise,

and whom we watch on that 'mild and golden September afternoon' loitering aimlessly among the graves of an old country churchyard. He finds the quiet of the spot soothing to nerves still a good deal shaken by the after-effects of illness, and by and by, as if piercing through the heavy deposit of years of monotonous business routine, and the perhaps still more monotonous routine of life with Sheila, its simple charm begins to elicit faint yet unmistakable responses from the day-dreaming boy, who ought in the nature of things to have been dead long ago. He certainly had *seemed* not only dead but buried; yet now he is stirring in his sleep, is giving startling and unaccountable manifestations of life. It is almost indeed as if they were walking hand in hand together along the silent paths, as if Lawford ever and again, responsive to a sudden small tug of that hand, were *obliged* to pause at this or that aspect in mild obedience.

So, the very first sentences, placing the scene, evoking the image of its stilled serenity, awaken also an indefinable thrill of expectancy, establish in our minds a conviction that the drama, the adventure, will be worked out on a spiritual plane.

[133]

Lawford has overestimated his strength, the pleasantness of the warm autumn day has tempted him to walk too far, and suddenly grown tired, he sits down beside an ancient grave near the low cypress-shaded wall, and after a little nods off to sleep there. Sheila would say—and indeed subsequently does say —that it was like him to choose, of all the graves, this particular tomb. For here, as it happens, many years ago had been laid the body of Nicholas Sabathier—an adventurer, a foreigner, who had died by his own hand, and who therefore *might*, as Lawford reflects, have been buried at the cross-roads with a stake thrust through his heart.

This is the first motif, the motif of the drowsy country churchyard, beautiful, peaceful, half reclaimed by nature. Again and again it rises like an incantation through the rich and tragic major theme, a spell calling the restless spirit to a dark and endless rest.

While Lawford sleeps, the eager ghost of the dead Huguenot—the only unquiet occupant of that remote and bird-haunted world—thirsting passionately for life once more, life at any price, makes an assault upon his defenceless visitor; and when the sleeper wakes the assault has been partially successful—not quite, for Lawford is still Arthur Lawford, though the enemy has gained a precarious footing within the citadel.

At first the signs of occupation are more physical than ghostly: Lawford himself is conscious of them only vaguely in an unaccustomed and very welcome sense of physical well-being that is almost like a return to youth: it is when the stranger seeks to establish a more complete mastery that the struggle between them becomes fierce and ruthless, till at last, consumed by the flame of that intenser life, the weakened body wearies, and a desire to surrender, a desire to end the battle, a longing unspeakable for the twilight, the green secrecy and silence of the grave, tempts him to accept defeat.

The life-and-death nature of this struggle is conveyed with an extraordinary intensity, but with the utmost restraint. It is very quiet, but it never relaxes. It is indeed a case of possession, though of incomplete possession. The hold of the dark sinister shadow against whom Lawford is fighting fluctuates, slips, misses, but the fighter is grimly, desperately in earnest. Already he has left scars and wounds on his antagonist, already he has gained ground, sufficient ground to make an attack on the external plane: the dim menacing form is half materialized, crouches, ready to spring at the slightest relaxing of his victim's over-taxed will.

Poor Sheila—distracted, humiliated, yet convinced—in despair sides against her husband. Come what may, she will not relinquish *her* world of respectable conventions and hallowed illusions, which somehow the very sight of Lawford now outrages. She feels that world growing ever more flimsy, and it is *his* fault, he *makes* her realize its insecurity, and how hollow their relation to each other has been for years. She shuts her eyes to reality; love isn't hollow, it is sacred, and she has always been fond of Arthur, has always done her duty. But there are limits to the sacrifices one can make —or at any rate can go *on* making—especially when it isn't only oneself who is concerned: in self-defence Sheila becomes unscrupulous.

As for Lawford, his mind and all his physical senses are sharpened to a quite new clarity and alertness. He feels the wild passionate stirrings of a new life within him—a longing for freedom, a longing for action; but the moral qualities of Sabathier have scarcely influenced him; he retains the Lawford moral sense with all its conscientiousnesses and prohibitions, though the passionate restless intelligence of his enemy has burned deeply in. And there are dreams and visions—sleeping dreams and waking visions—which are not the old stupid honest Lawford dreams, nor even the dreams of boyhood, but which come—beautiful, wild, desolating in their fierce longing and regret—from that dreadfully *other* memory.

He gazed idly down, listening vaguely to the wailing of a curlew flitting anxiously to and fro above the broken solitude of its green hill. And it seemed as if a thin and dark cloud began to be quietly withdrawn from over his eyes. Hill and wailing cry and barn and water faded out. And he was staring as if in an endless stillness at an open window against which the sun was beating in a bristling torrent of gold, while out of the garden beyond came the voice of some evening bird singing with such an unspeakable ecstasy of grief it seemed it must be perched upon the confines of another world. The light gathered to a radiance almost intolerable, driving back with its raining beams some memory, forlorn, remorseless, remote. His body stood dark and senseless, rocking in the air on the hillside as if bereft of its spirit. Then his hands were drawn over his eyes. He turned unsteadily and made his way, as if through a thick, drizzling haze, slowly back.

'What is that—there?' he said almost menacingly, standing with bloodshot eyes looking down upon Herbert.

But Herbert cannot help him; it is Grisel, Herbert's sister, who helps, and but for whom Lawford never would have won through. He

[137]

visits the brother and sister at their old haunted house by the Widder. This house is a living creation, and its dream-like image rises above the rapid stream that sweeps its walls, like a dark flower. There it is that Herbert roots out from among his ancient tomes a little book. in which Lawford sees a rough portrait print of Sabathier; there it is, in the dusky library above the sounding river, that he listens disconsolately to Herbert's too ready theories. For Herbert is clever and very friendly, but his sophistication matches ill with the simplicity of his racked and stricken companion, whose visible distress embarrasses him, so that he talks for talking's sake, throws out fantastic suggestions, drops them, contradicts them, trying to take back what he all too impulsively and recklessly has said on an earlier occasion. A note of insincerity strikes through Herbert's brilliant improvisations; their racy cheerfulness does not ring quite true; he is not sure of his ground; he talks too much. Lawford has a wiser friend in Mr. Bethany, the kind old parson, who from the beginning and by an act of the purest faith has ranged himself on his side.

Nevertheless, it is Grisel who saves him.

Grisel is young, beautiful—beautifully intelligent, and beautifully sympathetic. Is there perchance just the faintest hint that we may identify her with the lost love of Sabathier? I do not press the point; I don't know that I want it; for it is certain that the love which springs up between her and Lawford is no memory, no echo of an ancient passion. It is, on the woman's side, all tenderness and pity and generosity; and it is treated by the author with a supreme delicacy. It saves Lawford—it and, less explicitly, his love for his daughter Alice, who is still little more than a child. For he *is* saved. We leave him worn out and with but the feeblest hold on life, but saved, and saved moreover in a double sense, the second salvation being due to Sabathier himself. It was Sabathier who awakened his soul where it drowsed complacently in its stagnant prison; it was Sabathier who flung open the prison doors, letting in the air and light. Then the sluggish soul awoke—awoke in danger—but now the danger is past. Only, the new Lawford is very different from the old. From the old Lawford there never could have been wrung this cry in which the deepest depth of his tormented spirit is revealed.

'At death's door . . . who was it was saying that? Have you ever, Sheila, in a dream, or just as one's thoughts go sometimes, seen that door? . . . its ruinous stone lintel, carved into lichenous stone heads . . . stonily silent in the last thin sunlight, hanging in peace unlatched. Heated, hunted, in agony—in that cold, green-clad, shadowed porch is haven and sanctuary. . . . But beyond—O God, beyond!'

To which outburst poor Sheila makes a reply that all unconsciously has the effect of the most devastating cynicism.

In the later chapters Lawford has drawn strangely close to his creator; even in the earlier he was not intrinsically far from him: how else should he have been the medium through which we gain our vision of that haunted, darkly lovely world?

What is our final impression of *The Return*? The story takes us to the very brink of tragedy, but our last impression is not of tragedy unmixed. We do not know that the 'far-off desolate longing for home and childhood' which is its burden, is in the end frustrated: the book closes on an unanswered and surely unanswerable question. What we do know is that Lawford's battle is won. A spirit of deep gravity and tenderness rests on those final pages like a benediction: if of nothing else, they at least leave us convinced of the beauty of goodness.

This passionate spiritual beauty is the book's outstanding quality. Worthy of it is the writing—to my mind the most continuously beautiful prose Mr. de la Mare has given us. Let me quote this passage where Lawford, forsaken by Sheila and the servants, is alone in his own house late at night, and has been awakened by Mr. Bethany knocking at the hall-door.

He awoke and opened his eyes again on the gathering darkness of the great bedroom, and heard a quick, importunate, long-continued knocking on the door below, as of some one who had already knocked in vain.

Cramped and heavy-limbed, he felt his way across the room and lit a candle. He stood listening awhile: his eyes fixed on the door that hung a little open. All in the room seemed acutely, fantastically still. The flame burned dim, enisled in the sluggish air. He stole slowly to the door, looked out, and again listened. Again the knocking broke out, more impetuously and yet with a certain restraint and caution. Shielding the flame of his candle in the shell of his left hand, Lawford moved slowly, with chin uplifted, to the stairs. He bent forward a little, and stood motionless and drawn up, the pupils of his eyes slowly contracting and expanding as he gazed down into the carpeted vacant gloom; past the dim louring presence that had fallen back before him.

His mouth opened. 'Who's there?' at last he called.

'Thank God, thank God!' he heard Mr. Bethany mutter.

'I mustn't call, Lawford,' came a hurried whisper as if the old gentleman were pressing his lips to speak through the letter-box. 'Come down and open the door; there's a good fellow! I've been knocking no end of a time.'

'Yes, I am coming,' said Lawford. He shut his mouth and held his breath, and stair by stair he descended, driving steadily before him the crouching, gloating, menacing shape, darkly lifted up before him against the darkness, contending the way with him.

'Are you ill? Are you hurt? Has anything happened, Lawford?' came the anxious old voice again, striving in vain to be restrained.

'No, no,' muttered Lawford. "I am coming; coming slowly.' He paused to breathe, his hands trembling, his hair lank with sweat, and still with eyes wide open he descended against the phantom lurking in the darkness—an adversary that, if he should but for one moment close his lids, he felt would master sanity and imagination with its evil. 'So long as you don't get in,' he heard himself muttering, 'so long as you don't get *in*, my friend!'

'What's that you're saying?' came up the muffled, querulous voice; 'I can't for the life of me hear, my boy.'

'Nothing, nothing,' came softly the answer from the foot of the stairs. 'I was only speaking to myself.'

Deliberately, with candle held rigidly on a level with his eyes, Lawford pushed forward a pace or two into the airless, empty drawing-room, and grasped the handle of the door. He gazed in awhile, a black oblique shadow flung across his face, his eyes like an animal's, then drew the door steadily towards him. And suddenly some power that had held him tense seemed to fail. He thrust out his head, and, his face quivering with fear and loathing, spat defiance as if in a passion of triumph into the gloom.

Still muttering, he shut the door and turned the key. In

another moment his light was gleaming out on the grey perturbed face and black narrow shoulders of his visitor.

'You gave me quite a fright,' said the old man almost angrily. 'Have you hurt your foot, or something?'

'It was very dark,' said Lawford, 'down the stairs.'

'What!' said Mr. Bethany still more angrily, blinking out of his unspectacled eyes; 'has she cut off the gas, then?'

In form the novel is admirable: a single creative impulse runs through it, and the writer is completely in possession of every phase and aspect of his subject. From the first pages in which Lawford comes into view pottering among the tombs in Widderstone Churchyard, to the last where we leave him sleeping the sleep of utter exhaustion in his empty rain-washed house, while Mr. Bethany, like a faithful watch-dog, guards his slumbers, nodding his own wise old head, but quick at the slightest sound to awaken into protective alertness— from the first page to the last the story is drenched in an atmosphere that induces a state of complete receptivity, so that the mind of the reader responds to every subtlest vibration in the mind behind the work. Nor can I discover more than one tiny break in the continuity of method. It is of no importance, and occurs towards the end of the twentieth chapter, when —for a dozen lines which doubtless seemed

to the author necessary for perfect lucidity—
Herbert and his sister are momentarily confronted in the absence of Lawford. Mr.
Bethany's vigil on the last page of all is not
a break; it strikes beautifully a last echoing
chord, is a kind of epilogue, since the story,
before the vigil begins, is already over.

There remains that story, and it is of the
deepest interest. This interest, this excitement in fact, is a steadily increasing quantity;
the thing once started goes on of its own
impetus, gathering dramatic intensity as it proceeds. I have dwelt too exclusively, I dare say,
on the prolonged duel between the haunter and
the haunted, picking out the tune to the neglect
of its accompaniment, which is composed of all
the motley stuff of life. We see Lawford in
the *midst* of life, confronted by its stupidities,
meannesses, grossnesses, selfishnesses, as well as
by its loyalties, generosities, and faith. The
characters, from Lawford himself to Ada the
housemaid, without exception live. Every
scene rings true. The beautiful chapter where
Lawford goes at night to his daughter's room;
the eerie chapter where Sheila and her friends
discuss in more or less veiled terms how she is
to get rid of Lawford, while Ada, downstairs

in the kitchen, becomes conscious that some-
body who should *not* be there has entered the
house; the thrillingly dramatic chapter in
which Grisel helps him to fight past the churchyard where the menacing enemy awaits him
in the shadow; the pages in which old Miss
Sinnet calls to tell him of her encounter with a
mysterious stranger: all these have a power
and a reality, a terror or a beauty or a tenderness that pierces straight through to the
imagination.

The element of humour, never absent from
Mr. de la Mare's work, here manifests itself
chiefly as irony. From the nature of the subject it necessarily is held in restraint, but its
effect is constantly present in the self-revelations
of Sheila and her circle. Without humour
there can never be complete reality, and Sheila's
whole mental equipment is epitomized in the
preparation for her soul-racked husband of a
dish of cornflour. To her he is ill, and illness,
even if it is of this abnormal and odious kind,
is usually to be met, temporarily at least, with
slops. But before condemning Sheila we must
remember the extraordinarily difficult position
in which her very weakness of imagination and
total *lack* of humour place her. Her whole life

K

has been ruled by what other people think, and she can guess only too accurately what they will think of this reincarnation of Sabathier in her husband. To begin with, most of them won't believe he *is* her husband (the inexpressible Danton at least pretends he doesn't). Sheila, in fact, would give anything not to believe it herself. But she can't help believing it, and her conviction is accompanied by a scarcely repressed exasperation with Lawford for allowing such a thing to happen. She is certain it never would or could have happened to *her*, and at the back of her mind there hovers a vague suspicion that Lawford must have *done* something— something people don't do—respectable people at all events. How else could providence have permitted it? Such small cruelties are by no means impossible to Sheila: they rise like sharp little rocks through the calm of her despair: but there are moments when she really does try (inevitably in the wrong way) to make the best of a bad business. She even forces herself to view the case as perhaps not entirely unprecedented, but she 'hasn't studied such things'. ' "We were all very much restricted in our reading as children, and I honestly think, not unwisely. . . . I dare say even such an unheard-of thing as what we are discussing now, or something equally ghastly, does occur occasionally. In foreign countries perhaps." ' There is no denying the authenticity of Mrs. Arthur Lawford's conversation: in that tacit criticism of 'foreign countries' Sheila is there to the life.

CHAPTER IX

POEMS OF MATURITY

I. THE LISTENERS (1912); PEACOCK PIE (1913)

THE LISTENERS unquestionably places Mr. de la Mare among the greatest poets of childhood and dreamland. It is not so much that the field of his subject matter has greatly widened, as that his art has been perfected. Therefore, even though the theme should remain more or less an old theme, the achievement will be different; and actually we find several old themes revived. I may appear to be mixing up oddly poetry with prose, but does not such a poem as *Miss Loo* belong to that group of compositions which includes *Miss Duveen*, and in which we see a small boy in relation to an elderly person of eccentric mind and habit? and does not the poem I am about to quote repeat in verse a motif we found in *The Riddle*, in *The Return*, and in *Ding Dong Bell*?

[148]

Half-hidden in a graveyard,
   In the blackness of a yew,
Where never living creature stirs,
   Nor sunbeam pierces through,

Is a tomb, lichened and crooked—
   Its faded legend gone—
With but one rain-worn cherub's head
   Of mouldering stone.

There, when the dusk is falling,
   Silence broods so deep
It seems that every wind that breathes
   Blows from the fields of sleep.

   .   .   .   .

And, all else lost and faded,
   Only this listening head
Keeps with a strange unanswering smile
   Its secret with the dead.

What at once strikes us is that the critical, didactic, and objective pieces in the author's second volume have here no successors. We have nothing in the manner of the *Characters from Shakespeare*, nothing in the manner of *Goliath*, and there are no more sonnets. In *The Listeners* and *Peacock Pie* we never pass beyond the boundaries of a world the poet has by now made peculiarly his own:

What can a tired heart say,
Which the wise of the world have made dumb?
Save to the lonely dreams of a child,
   'Return again, come!'

—and much of the substance of these books is composed of 'the lonely dreams of a child'.

Much of the substance of *The Listeners*, I should say, for the mood of *Peacock Pie* is altogether lighter, gayer, and the poems in the two books have been deliberately chosen to present a contrast. Not that there is a persistently lonely or brooding note even in *The Listeners*. The shadow of regret is intermittent, and where it does fall the accent of graver reverie acquires an extraordinary tenderness.

Rachel sings sweet—
  Oh yes, at night,
Her pale face bent
  In the candle-light,
Her slim hands touch
  The answering keys,
And she sings of hope
  And of memories:
Sings to the little
  Boy that stands
Watching those slim,
  Light, heedful hands.
He looks in her face;
  Her dark eyes seem
Dark with a beautiful
  Distant dream;
And still she plays,
  Sings tenderly
To him of hope,
  And of memory.

Surely a soft flame shines delicately but very brightly through these lines, an emotion which we feel to be sacred. The beauty in this particular poem seems to me of a different kind from the beauty in any other poetry I know, because the emotion it expresses is of a different kind. The tune is a simple one, but its exquisite modulations make it like some old-fashioned air played by a great master; we are approaching, in fact, very near to the almost supernatural music of some of the lyrics in *Motley* and *The Veil*. And, to choose a poem more universal perhaps in its appeal, is not this brief epitaph as certain of immortality as anything that has been written in our time?

> Here lies a most beautiful lady,
> Light of step and heart was she;
> I think she was the most beautiful lady
> That ever was in the West Country.
> But beauty vanishes; beauty passes;
> However rare—rare it be;
> And when I crumble, who will remember
> This lady of the West Country?

The contrast in colour we find in *The Listeners* and *Peacock Pie* reminds us of the similar contrast noted in the two prose romances of 1910. To keep to our analogy, it is as if

the author deliberately had arranged his palette
as a painter does, using in *Peacock Pie* only
cool, clear, delicate tints, while the colour of
The Listeners is rich and sombre. In two or
three of these poems one becomes conscious of
a spiritual affinity with Edgar Poe. Of a mood
of spiritual affinity I should say, for it is really
no more than that. But in *Never-To-Be*, *The
Dark Château*, *The Dwelling-Place*, *Time Passes*
—in the imagery and symbolism of these—
though they are certainly de la Mare's own—
we catch glimpses of Poe's peculiar landscape.
Those dark castles and rotting towers rising
in 'far ravines' where 'dream-waters' descend
soundlessly to a 'shoreless sea', loom up as if
on the confines of the elder poet's kingdom.
Only, whereas in Poe such a background
or atmosphere forms part of the sole world
in which his lyrical genius can live and
breathe, in de la Mare it is but the expression of one mood among many. Here,
however, is a poem that is idiosyncratic with a
vengeance.

> While at her bedroom window once,
>   Learning her task for school,
> Little Louisa lonely sat
>   In the morning clear and cool,

She slanted her small bead-brown eyes
  Across the empty street,
And saw Death softly watching her,
  In the sunshine pale and sweet.

His was a long lean sallow face;
  He sat with half-shut eyes,
Like an old sailor in a ship
  Becalmed 'neath tropic skies.
Beside him in the dust he had set
  His staff and shady hat;
These, peeping small, Louisa saw
  Quite clearly where she sat—
The thinness of his coal-black locks,
  His hands so long and lean
They scarcely seemed to grasp at all
  The keys that hung between.
Both were of gold, but one was small,
  And with this last did he
Wag in the air, as if to say,
  'Come hither, child, to me!'

Louisa laid her lesson book
  On the cold window-sill;
And in the sleepy sunshine house
  Went softly down, until
She stood in the half-opened door,
  And peeped.   But strange to say,
Where Death just now had sunning sat,
  Only a shadow lay:
Just the tall chimney's round-topped cowl,
  And the small sun behind,
Had with its shadow in the dust
  Called sleepy Death to mind.

[153]

But most she thought how strange it was
Two keys that he should bear,
And that, when beckoning, he should wag
The littlest in the air.

This poem is called *The Keys of Morning*, and nothing Mr. de la Mare has written, I think, produces quite so extraordinary an effect of mingled fantasy and homeliness. It is more bizarre than uncanny; still there definitely is that slight shudder in it which after *The Listeners* almost disappears from his poetry. Equally definitely it is the poetry of magic. 'The sunshine pale and sweet' has literally the effect of an incantation: the word 'wag' is of enormous importance; I do not hesitate to say that it is the most important single word in the entire composition—certainly no other supplies so far-reaching an influence. And then, the Pre-Raphaelite detail makes the whole thing concrete and authentic.

This curiosity of observation, this interest and joy in the minutest details of earth's beauty, this Pre-Raphaelitism that notes the tiny spotted scarlet beetle like a bright jewel on the green blade of grass, Mr. de la Mare carries into the most visionary poems, giving them body and actuality. It is present, if less marked, in *The*

Listeners, the composition that of all he has written perhaps, with the exception of *The Riddle*, comes closest to a pure dream poem. Closest, because *The Listeners* is not, I think —is not at any rate unmistakably—a dream poem, but hovers between that and a poem of dreamland. The distinction is genuine.

> Softly along the road of evening,
>   In a twilight dim with rose,
> Wrinkled with age, and drenched with dew,
>   Old Nod, the shepherd, goes.
>
> His drowsy flock streams [1] on before him,
>   Their fleeces charged with gold,
> To where the sun's last beam leans low
>   On Nod the shepherd's fold.

—that is a poem of dreamland, but hardly a dream poem.

In connexion with this subject, and in connexion with one of his own most mysteriously beautiful lyrics, *The Cap and Bells*, Mr. W. B. Yeats has written a delightful note. 'I dreamed this story exactly as I have written it,' he says, 'and dreamed another long dream after it,

---

[1] I cannot resist alluding to the 'magic' or alchemical effect of the word 'streams'. Poetry, we must admit, does contain these runic words, though the secret of their power—which is anything but constant—may be unfathomable. All we can say is that they are ordinary words used imaginatively.

trying to make out its meaning, and whether I was to write it in prose or verse. The first dream was more a vision than a dream, for it was beautiful and coherent, and gave me the sense of illumination and exaltation that one gets from visions, while the second dream was confused and meaningless. The poem has always meant a great deal to me, though, as is the way with symbolic poems, it has not always meant quite the same thing. Blake would have said "the authors are in eternity", and I am quite sure they can only be questioned in dreams.'

Both *The Cap and Bells* and Coleridge's *Kubla Khan* are pure dream poems,[1] and so I should say, though it is closer to the logical continuity of our waking consciousness, is *The Riddle*. By which I mean that none of these things has been rationalized; the waking intellect has not consciously collaborated with the dream. *The Riddle* seems to have emerged just as it is out of the depths below sleep and to be addressed to the dream consciousness of the reader. In *The Listeners*, as in Poe's

[1] Another example of a dream poem is *The Blue Closet* in William Morris's *Defence of Guenevere*, where there are indeed several such things.

Ulalume, there has been to some extent a collaboration, an attempt to interpret, to throw a bridge across the dream fissures, to present the story in terms of logic. *The Listeners* is too well known to require quotation, but the dream is in the first eight lines of it: then follows an elaboration of the dream, and to the waking collaborator I should say we owe definitely the two lines:

'Tell them I came, and no one answered,
    That I kept my word,' he said.

I do not pretend that the poem actually was composed like this: I am only trying to describe an impression: but whether they are a later addition or not, the two lines I have quoted, to my sense at least, seem slightly out of key with the rest. They create a definite story by introducing a motive, that motive being the keeping of a tryst, and proportionately they limit the meaning and diminish the dream effect.

The Listeners is the most popular of all Mr. de la Mare's lyrics. It is very beautiful, but it is not the most beautiful he has written; it is musical, but not with his rarest music. Yet because of the extraordinary lilt and originality of its metrical scheme it has somehow caught

[157]

the popular taste, and there appears to be a
danger of its coming to occupy a position
among his poems not unlike that of *The Raven*
among the poems of Edgar Poe.

> 'Is there anybody there?' said the Traveller,
>   Knocking on the moonlit door;
> And his horse in the silence champed the grasses
>   Of the forest's ferny floor. . . . .

The swaying stresses of the long lines are drawn
into the melodic pattern by alternate lines of
regular and emphatic beat, the actual tune
being grasped by the ear at once.

This kind of syncopation, however, is not
confined to *The Listeners*. We get it in *The
Journey*:

> Heart-sick of his journey was the Wanderer;
>   Footsore and parched was he;
> And a Witch who long had lurked by the wayside,
>   Looked out of sorcery.

We get it in *Arabia*; even in *The Bandog*:

> Has anybody seen my Mopser?—
>   A comely dog is he,
> With hair of the colour of a Charles the Fifth
>   And teeth like ships at sea,
> His tail it curls straight upwards,
>   His ears stand two abreast,
> And he answers to the simple name of Mopser,
>   When civilly addressed.

The Bandog could hardly have been printed in *The Listeners*: it approximates to nonsense verse, though nonsense verse written by a poet. It has been placed, therefore, in *Peacock Pie*, which contains a good many things addressed directly to the nursery. They are of a different kind, some of these things, from the earlier rhymes for children. Behind even the lightest and slightest of the *Songs of Childhood* there can be detected an impulse that relates them to Mr. de la Mare's serious poetry; but in *Peacock Pie* this is not always so, the nursery pieces are in fact subject to an odd variation of tone. There are rhymes, like *The Huntsmen*, which are good, jolly rhymes and nothing more; but there are others, which also set out to be just good, jolly rhymes, and yet have somehow become poetry. Such, surely, is this exquisite little cameo taken from the same group.

> I heard a horseman
>   Ride over the hill;
> The moon shone clear,
>   The night was still;
> His helm was silver,
>   And pale was he;
> And the horse he rode
>   Was of ivory.

It is a nursery rhyme of course, but it is also

a poem that might have been written by the author of *Tom o' Bedlam*.

Peacock Pie has for sub-title 'a book of rhymes', as if therein lay an implicit avowal of its less serious intention: and yet some of it is serious poetry, and not all of it is even poetry of childhood. Things like *The Song of Shadows*, or *The Song of the Mad Prince*, are closely akin to the most beautiful lyrics in *Motley* and *The Veil*. Of those poems which stand half-way between the gaiety of *The Bandog* and the delicate, wistful loveliness of *The Mad Prince* I cannot resist quoting '*Sooeep!*'

> Black as a chimney is his face,
>   And ivory white his teeth,
> And in his brass-bound cart he rides,
>   The chestnut blooms beneath.
>
> 'Sooeep, Sooeep!' he cries, and brightly peers
>   This way and that, to see
> With his two light-blue shining eyes
>   What custom there may be.
>
> And once inside the house he'll squat,
>   And drive his rods on high,
> Till twirls his sudden sooty brush
>   Against the morning sky.
>
> Then 'mid his bulging bags of soot,
>   With half the world asleep,
> His small cart wheels him off again,
>   Still hoarsely bawling, 'Sooeep!'

Chimney-sweepers have always rewarded
their champions by inspiring them to write
delightfully, whether it is in the prose of Charles
Lamb or in the verse of Walter de la Mare:
little chimney-sweepers, that is to say, for, as
Charles points out, 'old chimney-sweepers are
by no means attractive'. Mr. de la Mare's
sweep is sufficiently grown-up to have a hoarse
voice, therefore he has not quite the endearing
quality of 'those tender novices, blooming
through their first nigritude, the maternal wash-
ings not quite effaced from the cheek—such as
come forth with the dawn, or somewhat earlier,
with their little professional notes sounding like
the *peep peep* of a young sparrow'. Always
they are seen, out of the poet's tenderness of
heart, in a clear morning world, though it must
sometimes be raining and winter. But the poet
sees them in the world he would like to give
them: it is as if, in imagination at any rate,
he would turn them loose in green summer
meadows, to sport in the deepest grasses and
under the bluest skies. Charles Kingsley gives
Tom in *The Water Babies* nothing less than the
whole fresh cool sparkling river for his home;
and in that wild gleaming light of a rapturous
innocence which floods the world of Blake's

L

little blackamoors, they seem to stand with their
naked feet bathed in the very dews of Paradise.

Peacock Pie and *The Listeners* as they were
originally issued are not entirely identical with
the *Peacock Pie* and *Listeners* of the *Collected
Poems*. From the former, *Up and Down,
Tillie*, and *Tit for Tat* have been omitted, while
a long poem, *Sam's Three Wishes*, has been
added. To *The Listeners* nothing has been
added, but the poet has rejected *Spring*, *Ages
Ago*, *Home*, and *The Witch*. This last delightful thing Mr. de la Mare once told me had
been left out by accident, though he now says
he told me nothing of the sort. However, I
give it, so that the reader himself may either
reject it in his turn, or restore it to its old place.

> Weary went the old Witch,
> Weary of her pack,
> She sat her down by the churchyard wall,
> And jerked it off her back.
>
> The cord brake, yes, the cord brake,
> Just where the dead did lie,
> And Charms and Spells and Sorceries
> Spilled out beneath the sky.
>
> Weary was the old Witch;
> She rested her old eyes
> From the lantern-fruited yew trees,
> And the scarlet of the skies;

And out the dead came stumbling,
From every rift and crack,
Silent as moss, and plundered
The gaping pack.

They wish them, three times over,
Away they skip full soon:
Bat and Mole and Leveret,
Under the rising moon;

Owl and Newt and Nightjar:
They take their shapes and creep,
Silent as churchyard lichen,
While she squats asleep.

All of these dead were stirring:
Each unto each did call,
'A Witch, a Witch is sleeping
Under the churchyard wall;

'A Witch, a Witch is sleeping . . .'
The shrillness ebbed away;
And up the way-worn moon clomb bright,
Hard on the track of day.

She shone, high, wan and silvery;
Day's colours paled and died;
And save the mute and creeping worm,
Nought else was there beside.

Names may be writ; and mounds rise;
Purporting, Here be bones:
But empty is that churchyard
Of all save stones.

Owl and Newt and Nightjar,
Leveret, Bat and Mole
Haunt and call in the twilight,
Where she slept, poor soul.

II. MOTLEY (1918); THE VEIL (1921); LATER POEMS [1]

Looking back from *The Veil* and the few poems he has published since *The Veil*, we can see, as from some hill-side commanding the way, how far Mr. de la Mare has journeyed and how rich in beauty and discovery the journey has been. It seems a long time since, like Henry Brocken, he first set out in the early morning to explore a new strange world. In those days Timothy and Ann were with him, the deliberate Lucy, the practical Jane. But where is that company now? No sight nor sound of them. The scene and the season too have altered; there are dead leaves on the ground and the sky is overcast.

And it is well. The old songs are always there. We have but to retrace the traveller's steps and we shall find Timothy and Jane waiting for us; hear Mary's twangling harp

[1] *Thus Her Tale* (1923), *A Ballad of Christmas* (1924), *Christmas* (1925), *Alone* (1927), *Self to Self* (1928), *The Captive and Other Poems* (1928).

and John's silver flute. These must remain for ever changeless; their clear day is not measured by our clocks; Lucy will still go a-walking, Jane still cheat the greedy wolf, long after their present lovers are grown indifferent to wolves and flutes alike. That bright gay company sang their last tunes in *Peacock Pie* perhaps (for the *Stuff and Nonsense* of 1927 does not count here); the altered, deeper note was already struck in *The Listeners*; it is intensified in *Motley*, which came six years later; and in *The Veil* it sounds more persistently still.

Not that the dream element, nor even the fantastic element, has ceased to exist. The very first poem of *Motley*, lovely thing that it is, is a fantasy, not quite in the old manner but breathing the old magic. The *Little Salamander* might indeed have been sung by Nod in the forests of Munza-Mulgar:

> When I go free,
> I think 'twill be
> A night of stars and snow,
> And the wild fires of frost shall light
> My footsteps as I go;
> Nobody—nobody will be there
> With groping touch, or sight,
> To see me in my bush of hair
> Dance burning through the night.

But the dreamer is disturbed by a knocking at the door that bids him waken, that calls him back to 'leaden day by day'. As I said in an earlier chapter, *The Veil* at any rate, if not *Motley*, in the field of its subject matter is more closely allied to the *Poems* of 1906 than to *The Listeners* and *Peacock Pie*. Even in *Motley* there are few stories, and no children; while in *The Veil* the creative spirit is working in a wholly different way and on a wholly different material, contemplation and interpretation having largely taken the place of picture and story. But the 'rhythmic creation of beauty' becomes even more marvellous; the fusion of form and substance is complete; and the poet, working in an altered mood and to a different end, is still the poet of dream and vision, of secret glades and beloved ghosts. In a sense, indeed, he is more this than ever, for never before was he so haunted by a longing for Paradise. It is because this poetry carries us perpetually beyond the world—this world where 'sin, and beauty, whisper of Home'—to a world of absolute beauty, that it means more to us than even the earlier poetry did. Call it by what name you like, it is the same beckoning, shining shore; it is the Heaven of Vaughan and

Traherne, it is Poe's 'distant Aidenn', and for Walter de la Mare any fragment of earth's beauty—the dew on the grass, a bird's song, a light in the evening sky—is sufficient to set his imagination winging its way thither. At such moments his thought turns to music and an ecstasy wakes out of it that is the very voice of the thirsting, questing, recognizing spirit. The music, at its best, surpasses the loveliest music he had written before. There is a new flexibility and subtlety in its rhythms, which linger, rise, drop, following a wavering sinuous course, like the tremulous fall of a snowflake which the wind catches, holds, and releases again.

'Who knocks?'   'I, who was beautiful,
    Beyond all dreams to restore,
I, from the roots of the dark thorn am hither,
    And knock on the door.'

'Who speaks?'   'I—once was my speech
    Sweet as the bird's on the air.
When echo lurks by the waters to heed;
    'Tis I speak thee fair.'

'Dark is the hour!'   'Ay, and cold.'
    'Lone is my house.'   'Ah, but mine?'
'Sight, touch, lips, eyes yearned in vain.'
    'Long dead these to thine . . .'

Silence.   Still faint on the porch
   Brake the flame of the stars.
In gloom groped a hope-wearied hand
   Over keys, bolts, and bars.

A face peered.   All the grey night
   In chaos of vacancy shone;
Nought but vast sorrow was there—
   The sweet cheat gone.

In the substance of this poem the new note, it may be, is still half disguised.   But listen to this; *The Old Men*:

Old and alone, sit we,
   Caged, riddle-rid men;
Lost to Earth's 'Listen!' and 'See!'
   Thought's 'Wherefore?' and 'When?'

Only far memories stray
   Of a past once lovely, but now
Wasted and faded away,
   Like green leaves from the bough.

   .   .   .   .   .

We speak not; trembles each head;
   In their sockets our eyes are still;
Desire as cold as the dead;
   Without wonder or will.

And One, with a lanthorn, draws near,
   At clash with the moon in our eyes:
'Where art thou?' he asks: 'I am here,'
   One by one we arise.

And none lifts a hand to withhold
A friend from the touch of that foe:
Heart cries unto heart, 'Thou art old!'
Yet, reluctant, we go.

I should like to set beside these verses another
poem about old men, this time by Mr. W. B.
Yeats—not with any foolish thought of measur-
ing beauty with a rule, but for another purpose.

I heard the old, old men say,
'Everything alters,
And one by one we drop away.'
They had hands like claws, and their knees
Were twisted like the old thorn trees
By the waters.
I heard the old, old men say,
'All that's beautiful drifts away
Like the waters.'

The theme is the same, but, though the form
too is of course wholly different, it is to a
difference of spirit I would point. Neither
poem is the expression of an explicit creed,
but it seems to me that the first is, potentially
at least, Christian, the second Pagan. And
this is what I have been approaching so circuit-
ously. There are lines in Mr. de la Mare's later
poems which express an emotion we must surely
call religious: there are even one or two entire
poems, like the beautiful *Before Dawn*, which

would awaken no surprise were one to come
on them in an anthology of devotional verse.
Am I trying to discover more than is actually
there, trying, instead of looking at what *is*
there, to peer on into the future? I do not
know.   Much that is there seems contradictory
enough if we are searching for a definite faith
or philosophy—such as we undoubtedly do find
in poets so different from each other as Yeats
and Wordsworth.   The faith in all things just,
lovely, pure, and of good report was visible in
Mr. de la Mare's writings from the beginning,
but it was never, even in the old days, accompanied by an assurance that 'God's in His
heaven—all's right with the world'.   Still less
in these last poems—wherein the question actually is asked—is there any permanent assurance
of that sort.   Rather, we follow the secret quest
of a soul burdened with a sense of loneliness,
doubtful as to whether the light that leads it on
is really more than the creation of 'sweet desire'.

> Take comfort, listen!
>   Once we twain were free;
> There was a Country—
>   Lost the memory. . . .
> Lay thy cold brow on hand,
>   And dream with me.

> Long hours there are,
>   When mutely tapping—well,
> Is it to Vacancy
>   I these tidings tell?
> Knock these numb fingers against
>   An empty cell?
>
> Nay, answer not.
>   Let still mere longing make
> Thy presence sure to me,
>   While in doubt I shake:
> Be but my faith in thee,
>   For sanity's sake.

And again:

> Think! in Time's smallest clock's minutest beat
> Might there not rest be found for wandering feet? . . .
>
> No, no. Nor earth, nor air, nor fire, nor deep
> Could lull poor mortal longingness asleep.
> Somewhere there Nothing is; and there lost Man
> Shall win what changeless vague of peace he can.

It is an austere comfort. Earth's beauty, for all its glory, is too transitory to awaken a happiness that does not swiftly turn to grief, and surely only a very chastened consolation can spring from the thought that, though love may perish with the perishing memory, the world will still be fair when our closed eyes are blind to it.

Oh, when this my dust surrenders
Hand, foot, lip, to dust again,
May these loved and loving faces
    Please other men!
May the rusting harvest hedgerow
Still the Traveller's Joy entwine,
And as happy children gather
    Posies once mine.

And then these brave words:

    Look thy last on all things lovely,
    Every hour.   Let no night
    Seal thy sense in deathly slumber
        Till to delight
    Thou have paid thy utmost blessing;
    Since that all things thou wouldst praise
    Beauty took from those who loved them
        In other days.

It is the philosophy of every wise man: it is, taken in its fullest meaning, the secret of life itself; but it is not optimism, and above all will it seem insufficient to the soul passionately aware of its exile from God.

Yet, if life after death is uncertain, so too is death—the death that is synonymous with annihilation. The ruined temple, amid the stones of which creeping things have made their homes, suggests not a final 'nothingness' but a perpetual and ever unanswerable question:

Towards what eventual dream
Sleeps its cold on,
When into ultimate dark
These lives shall be gone,
And even of man not a shadow remain
Of all he has done?

Life is in truth a riddle, 'an endless war 'twixt contrarieties'. Therefore,

Leave this vain questioning. Is not sweet the rose?
Sings not the wild bird ere to rest he goes?
Hath not in miracle brave June returned?
Burns not her beauty as of old it burned?
    O foolish one to roam
    So far in thine own mind away from home!

And more hopefully this note is repeated in another poem:

When music sounds, all that I was I am
Ere to this haunt of brooding dust I came;
While from Time's woods break into distant song
The swift-winged hours, as I hasten along.

It is the doctrine of Vaughan and Words-worth. Or is it?—for with de la Mare it expresses, rather, a desire, which only at rare moments passes into tremulous faith.

    'Are you far away?'
    'Yea, I am far—far;
    Where the green wave shelves to the sand,
    And the rainbows are;

[173]

And an ageless sun beats fierce
From an empty sky:
There, O thou Shadow forlorn,
Is the wraith of thee, I.'

'Are you happy, most Lone?'
'Happy, forsooth!
Who am eyes of the air; voice of the foam;
Ah, happy in truth.
My hair is astream, this cheek
Glistens like silver, and see,
As the gold to the dross, the ghost in the mirk,
I am calling to thee.'

'Nay, I am bound.
And your cry faints out in my mind.
Peace not on earth have I found,
Yet to earth am resigned.
Cease thy shrill mockery, Voice,
Nor answer again.'
'O Master, thick cloud shuts thee out
And cold tempests of rain.'

Still, in spite of all, a feeling remains with
us that a seed is stirring in the ground—a feeling
that belief, complete, final, may flower at any
moment. What emerges clearly is that the old
dreams of 'Arabia' no longer suffice, that those
drowsy syrups have lost potency to lull the
unresting spirit. They are, moreover, attended
by perils, and one powerful gnomic poem, *The
Imagination's Pride*, warns the dreamer who

would lure his lonely 'fantasy to its utmost scope' of the insidious fascination that turns to menace when pursued beyond the forbidden horizon:

> Nectarous those flowers, yet with venom sweet.
> Thick-juiced with poison hang those fruits that shine
> Where sick phantasmal moonbeams brood and beat,
> And dark imaginations ripe the vine.
> Bethink thee: every enticing league thou wend
> Beyond the mark where life its bound hath set
> Will lead thee at length where human pathways end
> And the dark enemy spreads his maddening net.

Nor can it be said that in the few still later poems which bring us down to the present day the veil has been further withdrawn. Uncertainty is still their key-note. Everywhere, from the hills and the streams and the woods, voices call; but they may be mocking voices, and are never the clear, assuring voices Wordsworth heard in Nature. So it might have been with some unrecorded child of Adam wandering near the impenetrable hedges of Eden, alone, hoping always to find an entrance to that place where once he was happy, but from which, he knows not why, he is now banished. While out of the tree, the snake, his father's enemy, watches him with bright unblinking eyes.

It will be understood that I have concentrated on the poetry that is furthest removed from the earlier poetry. There are things in *Motley* that are in the earlier manner; in *The Veil*, I think, nothing. But in *The Veil* we find, for the first time, poems which have been inspired by what one calls the 'realities' of life. The beautiful and extraordinary *Hospital* is· such a poem, though it actually belongs to both worlds. Those two very grim pieces, *In the Dock*, and *Drugged*, however, are direct impressions of reality. The material is gloomy, squalid, terrible: the murderer haled 'from his poisonous slum', standing at the iron rail, 'pallid, misshapen', gloating in 'beastlike trance'; the drugged dreamer 'inert in his chair', his bottle empty, 'his fire sunk low', his 'unsated mouth ajar', his attic swarming with nightmare horrors in the light of a guttering candle. Such material was not absent from several of the tales, but never before had it been made into a poem. Yet these poems have a power and beauty as authentic as the exquisitely delicate beauty of a thing like *The Moth*.

The Moth is printed in *The Veil*, but it had appeared earlier, in 1919, in *Flora*, Miss Pamela Bianco's book of drawings; and quite apart from its intrinsic qualities it has a peculiar interest.

> Isled in the midnight air,
> Musked with the dark's faint bloom,
> Out into glooming and secret haunts
>   The flame cries, 'Come!'
>
> Lovely in dye and fan,
> A-tremble in shimmering grace,
> A moth from her winter swoon
>   Uplifts her face:
>
> Stares from her glamorous eyes;
> Wafts on her plumes like mist;
> In ecstasy swirls and sways
>   To her strange tryst.

And now let me quote a passage from W. H. Hudson's *Book of a Naturalist*, published also in 1919, a passage which would seem to have been written very nearly at the same time.

Another surprisingly beautiful moth is the crimson underwing. Once only have I been able to observe this lovely moth flying about—and it was in a room! I was staying with friends at the Angler's Inn at Bransbury on the Test when one evening after the lamps were lit the moth appeared in our sitting-room and remained two days and nights with us in spite of our kind persecutions and artful plans for his expulsion. It was early September, with mild sunny days and misty or wet nights, and in the evening, when the room was very warm, we would throw the windows and doors open, thinking of the delicious relief it would be for our prisoner to pass out of that superheated atmosphere, that painful brightness, into his own wide, wet world, its darkness and silence and fragrance, and a mysterious signal wafted to him from a distance out of clouds of whispering leaves, from one there waiting for him.

A word as to the style of these last poems. The writing is always the writing of a great artist who has invented and brought to perfection his own idiom, but in *The Veil* I think one becomes conscious now and again of an increasing inclination to begin a sentence with a verb or an adjective. I do not deny that inversion is sometimes necessary to secure an emphatic beat on a first syllable, nor that it can be employed—as Mr. de la Mare himself frequently employs it—with admirable effect; but it is an effect accompanied by danger—the danger, that is to say, of the ear retaining it from one poem to another.

> 'Screamed the far sea-mew.'
> 'Bell-shrill the oyster-catchers.'
> 'Burned the sky.'
> 'Crashed the Atlantic.'
> 'White swirled the foam.'

All these occurring in a single poem of sixteen lines suggest that it is at least not a danger the

[178]

poet fears. I hasten to add that this poem, *Flotsam*, has been specially picked out as the most extreme (and indeed quite exceptional) example I could find.

CHAPTER X

MEMOIRS OF A MIDGET (1921) .

THE fourth novel, *Memoirs of a Midget*, is a far more elaborate work than its predecessors, and is even more different from them than they are from one another. The book was instantly successful: to go back to an old story, it really did 'wake up the libraries', and introduced the author to a public he had never before reached.

Brilliantly intellectual, daringly inventive as it is, with its dazzling contrast of tones and wider vision of life, or at least the wider area of life it covers, it would be easy to prove *The Midget* an altogether larger and in some respects more wonderful achievement than *The Return*. Certainly Mr. de la Mare could not have written it when he wrote *The Return*, and if that is to be our criterion, then the general consensus of opinion that it is his prose masterpiece is justified. It *does* mark an advance; moreover I am ready to admit that it is an

even more original work than *The Return*—
not more imaginative, but more surprising,
more unique. And there I pause. *The Return*, to my mind, occupies a position in the very
centre of Mr. de la Mare's prose work: the
subject of that novel happened particularly to
suit his peculiar genius, and the book happened
to be written at a period when all his gifts were
exactly balanced. It produces an impression
of spontaneity: it may not have been easy to
write but it has the *appearance* of having been
easy to write, and its appeal is immediate.
The Midget—brilliant and objective—is a
stimulus to the intellect, which it leaves alert
and critical; but the earlier book is a dark and
mysterious inspiration, the kind of thing that
is shaped primarily by intuition and emotion,
whereas it is obvious that in *The Midget* thought
and invention have everywhere been busy,
weighing, sifting, and planning, in clear daylight. *The Return*, in short, is essentially a
lyrical novel, and those with whom this quality
comes first will never prefer its successor, any
more than they will prefer *King Lear* to *Twelfth
Night* or *The Tempest*.

The drama in *The Midget* might be viewed
as the struggle between the individual and

society. I do not say that this, consciously, is the theme of the book, but both Miss M. and Mr. Anon represent the 'different' (not only in so far as this may coincide with their own particular difference, but the 'different' regarded generically, philosophically), while all the other characters represent the norm. It is not so much that the two midgets declare war against society as that society can find no place for them. Mr. Anon, contemptuously, yet furiously, turns his back on the world, accentuates *his* 'difference' by trying to live as if he were alone on a desert island: Miss M. is of another spirit. She refuses to yield to mere numbers. If this self-chosen people could show her even the ghost of an ideal by which it proposed to live it might be otherwise; but to bow down before a mere *similarity* of impulse, prejudice, and superstition—why should she do that?—and Miss M. fights her battle bravely. Unfortunately, though her enemies are for the most part only noisy, common, and futile; though, taken singly, each would prove but a feeble opponent; their unanimity of purpose is appalling—has the senseless crushing weight of the wheels of Juggernaut, and if the struggle ends in a kind of truce, it is they who dictate its terms.

It is more, then, than a love of strangeness and fantasy that has led Mr. de la Mare to choose a midget for protagonist. At the same time it is easy to see how the choice brings into existence a host of difficulties the writer of an ordinary novel, or of an allegorical satire such as *Gulliver's Travels*, is not called upon to face. In *Gulliver* the simple machinery of the fairy tale is taken over just as it stands, the scene is laid in remote unvisited isles, and the problem of the creation of credulity no more exists than it did for the author of *Jack and the Beanstalk*. But it is a problem of prime importance in the work we are now discussing. *The Midget* is neither a fairy story nor an allegory; it is a novel of modern life—seen, it is true, from a peculiar angle, but none the less dependent for success on the illusion of reality.

The scheme of the book, the idea behind it, makes it essential that the reader should be brought as quickly as possible into sympathy with Miss M., through whose mind he is to *watch* everything, and in whose heart he is to *feel* everything. If it is difficult, however, to make even a blind or a lame hero quite sympathetic (so impressionable are we to physical aspects), how much *more* difficult will it be in the present case. Just what Miss M.'s inches are is never stated in so many words. There are hints, but her immense labour in descending the stairs in Chapter Six calls up a somewhat different image from that suggested by comparisons with children in one or two later passages. The clearest indication is furnished in the following lines: .

A slim, stilted greyhound on one such visit stalked out from the lodge. Quite unaware of his company, I turned about suddenly and stared clean down his arched throat—white teeth and lolling tongue. It was as if I had glanced into the jaws of destiny. He turned his head, whiningly yawned, and stalked back into the shade.

We know the height of a greyhound, and Miss M.'s stature would thus appear to be fixed once for all.

The aspect of her physical abnormality is not glossed over; we are never permitted to forget it. Wild animals are friendly to her; a field mouse will doze contentedly in her lap; the domestics, however, share to some extent the sense of repulsion felt by Mr. Percy Maudlen and certain other humans: Henry, the admirable cat of Mrs. Bowater, is reluctant even to remain in the same room with her.

Alone. Only for a moment, though. Its mistress gone,

as fine a black cat as ever I have seen appeared in the doorway and stood, green-eyed, regarding me. To judge from its countenance, this must have been a remarkable experience.

I cried seductively, 'Puss.'

But with a blink of one eye and a shake of its forepaw, as if inadvertently it had trodden in water, it turned itself about again and disappeared. In spite of all my cajoleries, Henry and I were never to be friends.

Yet Miss M., so far from bearing malice, actually thinks of Henry when she is trying to decide, for Mrs. Bowater's satisfaction, whether Mr. Anon is a gentleman or not.

I thought of my father, of Mr. Waggett, Dr. Grose, Dr. Phelps, the old farmer in the railway train, of Sir Walter Pollacke, my bishop, Heathcliff, Mr. Bowater, Mr. Clodd, even Henry—or rather all these male phantoms went whisking across the back of my mind.

Percy Maudlen's distaste is expressed more spitefully if not more openly than Henry's. At the risk of offending a useful and influential aunt, the wealthy Mrs. Monnerie, who has taken up Miss M. with all the enthusiasm of the genuine collector, Percy cannot resist placing her in the same category as Cherry the lapdog, and other exotic and pampered recipients of his aunt's favour.

'And where is the toadlet?' I heard him drawl one afternoon as I was being carried downstairs by the light-footed

[185]

Fleming, on the padded tray which Mrs. Monnerie had had made for the purpose.

'The toadlet, my dear Percy, is about to take a little gentle exercise with me in the garden, and you shall accompany us. . . .'

Then, 'Hah!' cried Mrs. Monnerie in a large, pleasant voice, 'here *is* Miss M. Percy has been exposing a wounded heart, precious one. He is hurt because you look at him as if there were positively nothing more of him than what is there to see.'

'Not at all, Aunt Alice,' Percy drawled, with a jerk of his cane. 'It was for precisely the opposite reason. Who knows you ain't a witch, Miss M.? Distilled? Heavens, Aunt Alice! you are not bringing Cherry *too*?'

Yes, Cherry was coming too, with his globular eye and sneering nose. And so poor Percy, with a cold little smile on his fine pale features, had to accommodate himself to Mrs. Monnerie's leisurely pace, and she to mine, while Cherry disdainfully shuffled in our rear. We were a singular quartette, though there were only two or three small children in the palisaded garden to enjoy the spectacle; and they, after a few polite and muffled giggles, returned to their dolls.

Yet Miss M. makes her conquests, too. Apart from Sir Walter, and Mrs. Bowater, is there not her little pasha, whom she encounters in a railway train?

My spirit drank in this company. So rapt was I that I might have been a stock of wood. Gathered together in this small space they had the appearance of animals, and, if they had not been human, what very alarming ones. As long as I merely sat and watched their habits I remained unnoticed. But the afternoon sun streamed hot on roof

and windows: and the confined air was soon so dense with
a variety of odours, that once more my brain dizzied, and
I must clutch at Pollie's arm for support.   At this movement
the little boy who had more than once furtively glanced at
me, crouched wriggling back against his mother, and edging
his face aside, piped up into her ear, 'Mamma, is that
alive?' . . .

'Hush, my dear,' said the lady, no less intent but less open
in her survey; 'hush, look at the pretty cows!'

'But she *is*, mamma.   It moved.   I saw that move,' he
asseverated, looking along cornerwise at me out of his uptilted
face.

Those blue eyes! a mingling of delight, horror, incredulity,
even greed swam in their shallow deeps.   I stood leaning
close to Pollie's bosom, breathless and helpless, a fascinating
object, no doubt.   Never before had I been transfixed like
this in one congregated stare.   I felt myself gasp like a fish.
It was the old farmer in the corner who at last came to
my rescue.   'Alive! *I* warrant.   Eh, ma'am?' he appealed
to poor Pollie.   'And an uncommon neat-fashioned young
lady, too.   Off to Whipham Fair, I'll be bound.' . . .

'I *want* that, mamma,' whispered the child.   'I *want* that
dear little lady.   Give that teeny tiny lady a biscuit.'

At this new sally universal merriment filled the carriage.
. . .   My young admirer, much against his mother's inclination, had managed to fetch out a biscuit from her reticule
—a star-shaped thing, graced with a cone of rose-tinted
sugar.   Still crouching back like a chick under her wing, he
stretched his bribe out at arm's length towards me, in a pink,
sweat-sparked hand.   All this while Pollie had sat like a
lump beside me, clutching her basket, a vacant, flushed smile
on her round face.   I drew myself up, and supporting myself
by her wicker basket, advanced with all the dignity at my
command to the peak of her knees, and, stretching out my

hand in return, accepted the gift. I even managed to make him an indulgent little bow, feigned a nibble at the lump of food, then planted it on the dusty ledge beneath the carriage window.

A peculiar silence followed. With a long sigh the child hid his face in his mother's sleeve. She drew him closer and smiled carefully into nothingness. 'There,' she murmured, 'now mother's treasure must sit still and be a good boy. I can't think why papa didn't take—second-class tickets.'

'But nor did that kind little lady's papa,' returned the child stoutly. . . .

But now the sun had begun to descend and the rays of evening to stain the fields. We lŏitered on from station to station. To my relief Pollie had at last munched her way through the pasties and sweetmeats stowed in her basket. My nosegay of cherry-pie was fainting for want of water. In heavy sleep the bagman and gipsy sat woodenly nodding and jerking side by side. The lady had delicately composed her face and shut her eyes. The little boy slumbered serenely with his small red mouth wide open. Languid and heavy, I dared not relax my vigilance. But in the desolation that gathered over me I almost forgot my human company, and returned to the empty house which seemingly I had left for ever—the shadow of yet another nightfall already lengthening over its flowers and sward. . . .

I floated up out of these ruminations to find that my young pasha had softly awakened and was gazing at me in utter incredulity from sleep-gilded eyes. We exchanged a still, protracted, dwelling smile, and for the only time in my life I actually *saw* a fellow-creature fall in love!

'Oh, but mamma, mamma, I do *beseech* you,' he called up at her from the platform where he was taking his last look at me through the dingy oblong window, 'please, please, I want her for mine; I want her for mine!'

[188]

This, then, is the first task of the author—
to place the reader definitely on the side of the
pasha and not on that of Percy Maudlen.
Miss M. must be lovable to hold us; she must
have an attractiveness strong enough to out-
weigh our first instinctive distaste: all the fineness must be there, the delicacy and daintiness,
but with no hint of sickliness, no hint of
abnormality other than that accident of her
diminutive stature. And Miss M., too, must
live—live as a human being; she must be no
mere Titania enlivening a modern fairy tale;
her thoughts, her emotions, her sensations must
be convincing—removed ever so little from ours
(for she is different), rarefied ever so slightly,
but still remaining absolutely, deeply human,
and so open to the test of experience. Well,
Miss M. *does* live—lives so that we never for
an instant question her reality. We may at
times regret what she says or what she does
(her treatment of Mr. Anon is at the last a
trial, and a severe trial, of our affection), but
that she said those very things and did those
very things we *know*. And, somehow, she is
exquisite. Among her coarser earthmates—
gigantic, full-blown creatures—she is like a
harebell among peonies. She is all grace

and responsiveness, subtlety and intelligence,
though she can, with *her* human prejudices,
be obstinate, blind, and unfair. If she has set
her creator problems (which he has solved indeed, but which must have taxed all his skill),
she has also generously rewarded him. In the
delicate, clear mirror of her mind our jaded
dusty old world is reflected with a new and
radiant freshness; a bright, crystalline dew lies
upon it, sparkling and cool, and we see it as
on some lovely April morning. It is as if our
senses had been washed clean and we gazed not
only upon the earth but upon all its inhabitants
anew.

The book, as the title indicates, is Miss M.'s
autobiography, and the danger of the auto-
biographical form in fiction is that its elasticity
may become looseness, and its centre of interest
shift as one character after another crosses
the stage. Miss M. has this advantage over
the ordinary autobiographer, that the very
peculiarities of her position and point of view
in themselves tend towards unity of effect.
Moreover she never loses sight of the fact that
it is the *story* in her life she has set out to tell
us—*her* story, even when it becomes also Fanny
Bowater's. Her book holds together, it is com-

posed; though she has not tried (nor would it have been possible for her without sacrificing some of the material she proposed to use) to give it the firm shape of such a thing as *The Return*. One postulate, or convention, must be accepted from the start: namely, that she shares the genius of Mr. de la Mare. Miss M. is a poet, and there are moments when her autobiography, while still keeping in touch with the world around her, awakens a whispered echo from beyond. This echo sounds more intermittently than in the two earlier novels; sometimes, in fact, it is silent for quite a long time: and then, suddenly, at a turn of the page, once more we hear it.

She is completely free from sentimentality and self-pity. The story she tells is sometimes harsh, sometimes painful; its shadows deepen as it proceeds; but from the beginning it teems with an observation that is ironic, bold, and independent. It is, of course, in great measure the story of the world she watches with such brave steadfast eyes —the world she is 'up against', the world containing Mrs. Monnerie, Fanny Bowater, and Mr. Crimble, the tragic curate, whose body is 'found at 11.27 p.m. in an outhouse at the foot of his mother's garden'; but it is always, as I say, her own private story too, and is passionate enough, varied enough, exciting enough to hold us spell-bound. The people in it, shown as in actual life only through what they say and what they do, have passed—with perhaps one exception—through a creative imagination that has breathed into each an individuality and a soul.

The exception is Fanny Bowater. Fanny, in spite of the large place she occupies in the novel, presents always a hard, glittering, impenetrable surface to Miss M., so that for us, too, she remains to the end an enigma. But how well we get to know Mrs. Bowater, the landlady, with her bony hands, her 'long, springside boots', her 'thin hair sleekly parted in the middle over the high, narrow temples', her 'long, dark face with its black, set eyes'. Merely from this physical description we recognize that Mrs. Bowater belongs to Mr. de la Mare's world as well as to the Midget's: and it is perhaps the book's greatest triumph that from first to last it *is* the Midget's world we live in. Mrs. Bowater, however—unlike Fanny, unlike Mrs. Monnerie, unlike Percy Maudlen and Mr. Crimble—is a typical de la Mare character, in that we can see her ghost as well as her body. She strikes us, I mean, as the kind of person who is likely to 'come back'—though goodness knows *her* hauntings, kindly soul that she is, would be innocent enough.

What, then, are we to say of Mr. Anon? Mrs. Bowater after all, in spite of the atmosphere she trails with her, might have been 'observed', but Mr. Anon, we feel, has had no earthly progenitor, is the immediate creation of genius. He is a dwarf, a hunchback, a tragic human failure; but if we never lose consciousness of this, it is not what chiefly impresses us, because he is also a spirit, the spirit of the woods of Wanderslore. Rightly we are told nothing of his past, of his unhappy childhood and embittered youth. He has no name, no relatives, no friend. Actually he comes but seldom into the book; he does not come into it at all before the twenty-second chapter; and yet, from his first appearance, 'standing there, with fixed, white face and black hair, under a flowering blackthorn', he seems to fill it. From that moment we never forget him, never cease to look forward to his reappearance; his remembered image for us as for Miss M. is 'like that of one of those strange figures which thrust themselves as if out of the sleep-world into the mind's wakefulness; vividly, darkly impress themselves upon consciousness, and then are gone'. All the scenes where he is present are haunted. He is not only the spirit of Wanderslore, he is also the dark and passionate spirit of tragic love. I can think of no other writer except Emily Brontë who might have imagined him, or who could have drawn him with this strange certainty out of the unknown into our grosser, everyday world. Did Miss M. love him? She does not tell us. Not in life, perhaps, but I think afterwards. And there is a chance—perhaps more than a chance—that he was the Stranger of the prologue—the Stranger whom Mrs. Bowater heard but did not see, and after whose mysterious visit to Miss M. that little lady herself was never more to be seen by earthly eyes. We know there was a time when she did *not* love him: in fact, the only passionate love we watch awakening in her is lavished on the beautiful, fascinating, treacherous Fanny. Nevertheless, is not our impression of Mr. Anon Miss M.'s own impression—after tardy understanding had shown him at last and too late as by far the most lovable person she had ever met? Brilliant Fanny was the least. Therein lies the irony and cruelty of the Midget's fate. Like turns to unlike, and happiness is impossible.

Fanny, I must confess, I fail to understand. She is intended to be meretricious, but it is *essential*, in connexion with the effect she produces on more than one person in the novel, that she should have charm, and for me that charm does not come through, I have to take the author's word for it. Fanny is clever, *that* is plain, but her cleverness is so irritatingly self-conscious that it influences even poor little Miss M.'s own conversation when she is with her, as in the slightly strained scene where they go star-gazing together. Miss M.'s infatuation for the brilliant and elusive school-teacher, in short, has not sufficient foundation in the Fanny we see: I cannot help feeling our Midget—from what we know of her in other relations—falls in love too rapidly, too completely, or perhaps I should say with too little provocation. There is always Fanny's beauty of course, but everything else about her is *unattractive*; and is physical beauty alone sufficient explanation in this particular case, amply as it may account for the subjection and eventual suicide of Mr. Crimble, whose 'rather full red lips' and voice that reminded the Midget of raspberries are all so much to the good where an understanding of *his* affection is concerned? Fanny, for me then, remains a brilliant shadow, and her strange talk sets the seal upon her unreality. She is cold, devoid of sensuality for all her taste for philandering, devoid indeed of every feeling except resentment, cruelty, and the lust for power. She is meant to be complex, but what really baffles us is that we lack the clue to her changing moods; which means, I suppose, that Miss M. never possessed it. Her purpose in the novel is to bring disaster to those who care for her, and this at least she achieves, a trail of disillusionment and tragedy follows in her wake. For that matter, quite apart from Fanny, there is little happiness for anyone. 'It is not the ghosts of the dead and the past which I think should oppress the people I see around me,' writes Miss M., 'but those of the children to come. I thank God from the bottom of my heart for the happiness and misery of having been alive, but my small mind reels when I brood on what the gift of it implies.'

And it is in key with the universal irony of life that Miss M. herself, to whom so many

tactless, callous, stupid people have brought
suffering, should, in her turn, bring little else
to the one being who deeply loved her. Love,
in these *Memoirs*, is like a tiny gush of water
dropped on a burning desert: it is its own
reward perhaps; but no requital in kind attends
it. Is there any love here, from the pasha's
to Mr. Anon's, which is not wasted? Mrs.
Bowater's romance ended in desertion; Mr
Crimble's ends when he cuts his throat; Percy
Maudlen's will end the moment after he and
Fanny have signed their names in the vestry;
Miss M.'s ends when she reads the hatred in
Fanny's face; Mr. Anon's ends in the useless
sacrifice of his life.

What is the meaning of it all? Miss M. gives
us no answer. Nod, after toil, hardship, and
danger, reached the Valleys of his Tishnar;
but to keep what ultimate tryst did the Midget
go out? 'All that I write,' she herself says,
'is an attempt only to tell, not to explain.' Yet
sometimes the very telling seems to tremble
on the verge of explanation, and nowhere do
we feel such a revelation to be nearer than in
that beautiful evening scene at Wanderslore,
when the Midget has returned from her fine
London friends and has come out to meet,

almost for the last time, her truculent yet strangely gentle lover.

And in the silence, stealthily, out of a dark woody hollow nearer the house, as if at an incantation, broke a low, sinister, protracted rattle, like the croaking of a toad. I knew that sound; it came straight out of Lyndsey—called me back.

'S-sh!' I whispered, caught up with delight. 'A nightjar! Listen. Let's go and look.'

I held out my hand. His sent a shiver down my spine. It was clammy cold, as if he had just come out of the sea. Thrusting our way between the denser clumps of weeds, we pushed on cautiously until we actually stood under the creature's enormous oak. So elusive and deceitful was the throbbing croon of sound that it was impossible to detect on which naked branch in the black leafiness the bird sat churring. The wafted fragrances, the placid dusky air, and, far, far above, the delicate, shallowing deepening of the faint-starred blue—how I longed to sip but one drop of drowsy mandragora and forget this fretting, inconstant self.

We stood listening; and an old story I had read somewhere floated back into memory. 'Once, did you ever hear it?' I whispered close to him, 'there was a ghost came to a house near Cirencester. I read of it in a book. And when it was asked, "Are you a good spirit or a bad?" it made no answer, but vanished, the book said—I remember the very words—"with a curious perfume and most melodious twang." With a curious perfume,' I repeated, 'and most melodious twang. There now, would you like *me* to go like that? Oh, if I were a moth, I would flit in there and ask that old Death-thing to catch me. Even if I cannot love you, you are part of all this. You feed my very self. Mayn't that be enough?'

His grip tightened round my fingers; the entrancing, tone-less dulcimer thrummed on.

I leaned nearer, as if to raise the shadowed lids above the brooding eyes. 'What can I give you—only to be your peace? I do assure you it is yours. But I haven't the secret of knowing what half the world means. Look at me. Is it not *all* a mystery? Oh, I know it, even though they jeer and laugh at me. I beseech you be merciful, and keep me what I am.'

So I pleaded and argued, scarcely heeding the words I said. Yet I realize now that it was only my mind that wrestled with him there. It was what came after that took the heart out of me. There came a clap of wings, and the bird swooped out of its secrecy into the air above us, a moment showed his white-splashed cinder-coloured feathers in the dusk, seemed to tumble as if broken-winged upon the air, squawked, and was gone. The interruption only hastened me on.

'Still, still listen,' I implored: 'if Time would but cease awhile and let me breathe.'

'There, there,' he muttered. 'I was unkind. A filthy jealousy.'

'But think! There may never come another hour like this. Know, know now, that you have made me happy. I can never be so alone again. I share my secretest thoughts—my imagination with you; isn't that a kind of love? I assure you that it is. Once I heard my mother talking, and sometimes I have wondered myself, if I am quite like—oh, you know what they say: a freak of Nature. Tell me; if by some enchantment I were really and indeed come from those snow mountains of yours, and that sea, would you recognize me? Would you? No, no; it's only a story—why even all this green and loveliness is only skin deep. If the old world were just to shrug its shoulders, Mr. Anon, we should all, big and little, be clean gone.'

[199]

My words seemed merely to be like drops of water dripping upon a sponge. 'Wake!' I tugged at his hand. 'Look!' Kneeling down sidelong, I stooped my cheek up at him from a cool, green mat of grass, amid which a glow-worm burned: 'Is this a—a *Stranger's* face?'

He came no nearer; surveyed me with a long, quiet smile of infinitely sorrowful indulgence. 'A Stranger's? How else could it be, if I love you?'

Intoxicated in that earthy fragrance, washed about with the colours of the motionless flowers, it seemed I was merely talking to some one who could assure me that I was still in life, still myself. A strand of my hair had fallen loose, and smiling, its gold pin between my lips, I looped it back. 'Oh, but you see—haven't I told you?—I can't love you. Perhaps; I don't know. . . . What shall I do? What shall I say? Now suppose,' I went on, 'I like myself *that* much,' and I held my thumb and finger just ajar, 'then I like *you*, think of you, hope for you, why, that!'—and I swept my hand clean across the empty Zenith. '*Now* do you understand?'

'Oh, my dear, my dear,' he said, and smiled into my eyes. I laughed out in triumph at the success of my device. And he laughed too, as if in a conspiracy with me—and with Misery, I could see, sitting like an old hag at the door from which the sound came. And out of the distance the nightjar set again to its churring.

'Then I have made you a little—a little less unhappy?' I asked him, and hid my face in my hands, in a desolate peace and solitude.

He knelt beside me, held out his hand as if to touch me, withdrew it again. All presence of him distanced and vanished away in that small darkness. I prayed not to think any more, not to be exiled again into—how can I explain my meaning except by saying—Myself? Would some further world have withdrawn its veils and have let me in then and for ever if that lightless quiet could have continued a little longer? Is it the experience of every human being seemingly to trespass at times so close upon the confines of existence as that?

It was his own harsh voice that broke the spell. 'Wake, wake!' it called in my ear. 'The woman is looking for you. We must go.'

My hands slipped from my face. A slow, sobbing breath drew itself into my body. And there beneath evening's vacancy of twilight showed the transfigured scene of the garden, and, near me, the anxious, suffering face of this stranger, faintly greened by the light of the worm.

'Wake!' he bade me, rapping softly with his bony finger on my hand. I stared at him out of a dream.

No; there is no writing quite like this in *The Return*, no writing like it earlier than *Motley* and *The Veil*: but then, it is a marvellous passage even in *The Memoirs*; as I have said, all the scenes where Mr. Anon is present turn to poetry.

At this point we are nearing the close of Miss M.'s period of storm and stress, of seeking, finding and losing. *The Memoirs* are actually written years afterwards, and cover only the first two decades of her life. When she goes back to London after that strange hour at Wanderslore, it is to break for ever with Mrs. Monnerie and her fashionable friends. They are tired of her and she is sick of them. There is the brief, terrible experience of a travelling circus, and then the last meeting with Mr. Anon, in which she sacrifices him to pride, vanity, obstinacy. It may be harsh to blame her, for there was *his* pride too, *his* obstinacy: and yet we feel, when she lets him take her place and ride clumsily into the circus ring, almost as if she were deliberately sending him to his death. She sends him, at any rate, to be hooted, jeered at, insulted. And the disaster happens; the vicious little pony, maddened by the uproar of a hostile mob, throws him heavily. She knows he is hurt, but only gradually learns how much he is hurt, as they drive back through the dark cool night to Wanderslore.

Faint questions rise to her lips:

'Listen, tell me,' I entreated, 'you fell? I heard them calling and—and the clapping, what then?' I could speak no louder, but he seemed scarcely able to hear me.

'My shoulder,' he answered thickly, as if the words came sluggishly and were half-strange to him. 'I fell. . . . Nothing: nothing. Only that I love you.'

The breath sighed itself away. I leaned my cheek against the unanswering hand, and chafed it with mine. Where now? Where now?

'We must keep awake,' I called beguilingly into the slumbrous face, after a long silence, as if to a child. 'Awake!'

A sigh, as he smiled in answer, shook him from head to foot.

'You are thirsty? What's this on your coat? Look, there is a gate. I'll creep through and get help.' I scrambled up, endeavouring in vain to clutch at the reins.

But no; his head stirred its No; the left hand still held them fast. 'Only . . . wait.'

Was it 'wait'—that last faint word? It fell into my mind like a leaf into a torrent, and before I could be sure of it, the sound was gone.

Instinct, neither his nor mine, guided us on through the winding lanes, up hill and down, along the margin of sleeping wood and light-dappled stream, over a level crossing whose dew-rusted rails gleamed in the moon, then up once more, the retreating hill-side hollowly echoing to every clap of hoof against stone. There was no strength or will left in me, only thoughts which in the dark within, between waking and sleeping, seemed like hovering flies to veer and dart—fantasies, fragments of dream, rather than thoughts.

I realized how sorely he was hurt, yet not then in my stupidity and horror—or is it that I refused to confess it to myself?—that his hurt was mortal. Morning would come soon.

But morning, for Mr. Anon, never comes again. Nor is there any good-bye, any last word.

Once, I remember, I rose and threw my cape over his shoulder. At last I must have slept.

For the next thing I became conscious of was that the cart was at a standstill, and that the pony stood cropping the thyme-sweet turf by the wayside. I touched the cold dark hand. 'Hush, my dear, we are here!'

But I expected no answer. The head was sunken between the heavy shoulders; the pallid features were set in an empty stare.

[203]

They are home. She leaves the broken body to the care of others; and to us, too, it seems she has little right to care for it.

That last scene is incomparable in its tragic power and pathos. The book is over. In the few remaining pages we watch Miss M. drawn back, as through a lengthy convalescence, into a world more peaceful and more colourless.

How long she survived her lover Sir Walter Pollacke's brief introduction does not say. A good many years, the autobiography itself tells us. She had time, at least, to regain her customary busy and inquiring habit of mind, time to write the *Memoirs*, but it is significant perhaps that she found nothing in the events of her later life that seemed worth recording.

And so we leave her, conscious that she has brought us a long distance on our journey, but not yet, I think, within sight of the end; for, as I said in an earlier chapter, there are hints that that desolating scene of the return to Wanderslore is not fated really to be the end.

CHAPTER XI

THE LATER TALES (1921–1926)

CROSSINGS (1921); THE RIDDLE (1923); BROOM-
STICKS (1925); TWO TALES (1925); THE CON-
NOISSEUR (1926); AT FIRST SIGHT (1928);
UNCOLLECTED TALES

I

THE MIDGET must be nearly twice as long
as any of Mr. de la Mare's previous novels,
and while he was at work on it he kept closely
to his task. The method of work was, as usual,
to go over each morning what had been done
the day before, and then start out afresh from
that. In this way *The Midget* was written out
twice in longhand before the final typescript for
correction was made, yet the whole thing was
completed within ten months, a prodigious
example of sustained intellectual energy.

The completion of it left the author free to
return to the short story, and there followed a
harvest of tales of various kinds and importance.

These later stories, comprised in the volumes mentioned at the top of the previous page, with a few not yet collected in book form, I propose to discuss in a single chapter, though I must make a selection from them, and for the sake of convenience shall divide them (very loosely) into four groups.

To the first group I allot those stories in which the subjects are drawn from real life and kept there.

In Group Two I place the six tales of the supernatural—*Seaton's Aunt*, *Out of the Deep*, *All Hallows*, *The Green Room*, *A Recluse*, and *Miss Jemima*. The reader, I dare say, may be surprised that this group is not larger, and of course there are many children's stories that have to do with magic and fairies, but that is not just the same thing. In these lighter tales the author is playing with ideas that in the stories of our second group he takes seriously; their aim is but to beguile the fancy, and I shall regard them therefore as constituting Group Three, which, on the whole, I consider to be the least important section of Mr. de la Mare's work. Even that lovely little play, *Crossings*, must be relegated to this group, since the supernatural element in it does not proceed from, and is not addressed to, the deeper, questioning imagination, but is introduced solely for an artistic purpose—to charm, to amuse.

Our fourth and widest group is more difficult to define. The stories in it, when they are stories at all, hover on the edge of a world that is neither dreamland nor matter-of-fact. Such things as *The Creatures, Visitors, The Tree, Maria Fly*, would, we feel, be fairy stories if they weren't something quite different—something that is rooted in reality.

One of the very last things that Tom Nevis was to think about in this world was a sight he had seen when he was a child of about ten. Years and years were to pass by after that March morning; and at last Tom was far away from home and England in the heat and glare of the tropics. Yet this one far-away memory floated up into his imagination to rest there in its peace as a planet shining in its silver above the snows of remote hills. It had just stayed on in the quiet depths of his mind—like the small insects that may be seen imprisoned in lumps of amber, their wings still glistening ages after they were used in flitting hither and thither in their world as it then was.

Most human beings have little experiences similar to Tom's. But they come more commonly to rather solitary people—people who enjoy being alone, and who have day-dreams.

So begins the quaint and charming tale called *Visitors*, and it is, one suspects, just such little experiences that many of the compositions in

Group Four commemorate. The characters too, I should say, are as a rule drawn from within. Often the story is of the slightest, but the author has so keen a sense of everything that is touching, humorous, picturesque, or poetic in it, he bathes it in such a richness of tone and fills it out with such a wealth of meaning, that we ask for nothing more. In such things as *Disillusioned, The Vats, The Creatures, Alice's Godmother, Selina's Parable*, there is positively no story at all in the ordinary sense. I do not dare to suggest that this is partly why we return to them so often, but we really do get a fuller, and sometimes even a different impression from each renewed excursion into their quiet paths. To mention the subjects of these tales may throw a light on the author's mind, but very little on the tales themselves. A momentary flash of sympathy between an eminent physician and the patient who has come to consult him (*Disillusioned*); the sight of two vast primeval cisterns on an empty plain (*The Vats*); a glimpse of two slightly but far from unpleasantly abnormal children on a lonely farm (*The Creatures*); a farmyard on a summer afternoon (*Selina's Parable*): these are the 'insects' imprisoned in the amber of memory and imagination. *Disillusioned* consists primarily in what is left *unsaid* during a strangely suggestive but non-committal conversation: the effect of *Lispet, Lispett & Vaine* depends largely on our grasping the fact that Maunders is *improvising* the whole thing: the author of such tales surely is paying the highest compliment he can to his reader's intelligence. As for *The Thief*, it is less a story than an early Flemish picture glowing in jewelled colours: Bloudie Jacke of Shrewsberrie possessed no rarer collection.

II

'The real represents to my perception the things we cannot possibly *not* know, sooner or later, in one way or another; it being but one of the accidents of our hampered state, and one of the incidents of their quantity and number, that particular instances have not yet come our way. The romantic stands, on the other hand, for the things that, with all the facilities in the world, all the wealth and all the courage and all the wit and all the adventure, we never *can* directly know; the things that can reach us only through the beautiful circuit and subterfuge of our thought and our desire.'

The author of this passage can readily be

guessed, and while, as a definition, it does not cover the whole ground, since there is also a habit of mind, a point of view, we can only call romantic (Conrad's, for instance, who rarely if ever wrote of what he did not 'directly know'), it may at least serve to introduce the particular group of Mr. de la Mare's tales I have described as tales of real life. If those we shall discuss later stand, in Henry James's words, 'for the things that, with all the facilities in the world, we never can directly know, the things that can reach us only through the beautiful circuit and subterfuge of our thought and our desire', these —containing, among one or two minor pieces, *The Lost Track*, *Disillusioned*, *At First Sight*, *The Nap*, *Pretty Poll*, *Mr. Kempe*, and *Missing* —are composed of material quite within the grasp of experience. True, the subject of one of them, *Mr. Kempe*, has the strangeness, the fearful allurement of the abnormal (*Mr. Kempe* is the study of a disordered mind), but it is only an accident if Mr. Kempe or some one like him has not yet come our way: as for Mr. Bleet, the hero of *Missing*, he is not only sane but a person of marked sobriety, who, we can easily imagine, would be highly censorious of any infraction of social conventions.

Missing is among Mr. de la Mare's master-pieces. It is not a pleasant story, and it is remarkable that its sinister quality springs largely from its reticence. Mr. Bleet tells his interlocutor nothing alarming; Mr. Bleet is a victim of circumstances fortuitous and hostile. A chance encounter on a stifling Saturday after-noon in a second-rate London tea-shop having provided him with a confidant, he simply takes advantage of the fact. It is the confidant who describes their meeting.

I gave my order, and sat back exhausted in a listless vacancy of mind and body. And my dazed eyes, having like the flies little of particular interest to settle on, settled on the only fellow reveller that happened to be sitting within easy reach. At first glimpse there could hardly be a human being you would suppose less likely to attract attention. He was so scru-pulously respectable, so entirely innocent of 'atmosphere'. . . .

He wore a neat—an excessively neat—pepper-and-salt tweed suit, the waistcoat cut high and exhibiting the points of a butterfly collar and a triangle of black silk cravat slipped through a gold mourning ring. His ears maybe were a little out of the mode. They had been attached rather high and flat on either side of his conical head with its dark, glossy, silver-speckled hair.

The nose was straight, the nostrils full. They suggested courage of a kind; possibly, even, on occasion, bravado. He looked the kind of man, I mean, it is well to keep out of a corner. But the eyes that were now peering vacantly down that longish nose over a trim but unendearing moustache at the crumbs on his empty plate were too close together. . . .

Those eyes gave this spruce and respectable person just a hint, a glint of the fox.

And one or two other little physical peculiarities become apparent—the *glitter* in the 'close-neighbouring eyes', the hands, powerful and hairy.

What follows is an interesting talk in which Mr. Bleet, who has been rather deprived of companionship of late, does most of the talking. His listener has time to speculate, and the result somehow for us is that Mr. Bleet's conversation assumes a more and more ghastly complexion, while behind it we watch a soul, tormented, half-developed, and singularly unprepossessing.

The technique of the thing is superb; it is impossible to say at what moment our first vague suspicions of Mr. Bleet turn to certainties. The fatal word is never mentioned by either him or his companion, but no detailed description of an unusually savage murder could produce quite the dire effect of Mr. Bleet's picture of a blameless life in that 'nice little place' 'about seventy miles from London', where he resided with a half-witted sister and a paying guest, the buxom and comparatively opulent Miss Dutton.

The story is terrible, because below all that

is being said the spirits of both narrator and
listener are shuddering away from a glimpse of
some awful thing their words deny. On the
face of it, Mr. Bleet treats his companion to
no more than a spectacle of self-pity, broken
by an occasional outburst of resentment or
defiance. But he is not an engaging person
naturally, nor would be even had he happier
memories of which to unburden himself
than his tortuous and cautious account of
the 'Enquiry'. The 'Enquiry' was concerning
Miss Dutton, who was 'missing'. Yet even the
'Enquiry', for all its callousness, never went so
far as to mention murder. Moreover Mr. Bleet
completely cleared himself, we gather; left that
room without a stain on his character: except,
of course, in the jaundiced view of the
obstinately malicious, who unfortunately comprised the majority of his neighbours. He
clears himself anew on this breathless, enervat-
ing afternoon; and at the same time there grows
up in the thickening air behind him a scene
that becomes more and more vivid with every
indignant protest he utters—a picture of a
deliberate but ferocious act, and of all the grisly
business connected with the subsequent disappearance of Miss Dutton—a picture of Miss

Dutton herself, or rather of her remains, a little
messy now, but still plump, blonde, slightly
common though 'quite the lady'—of her very
clothing. And, I repeat, not one word of these
things exists on the printed page.

What does exist is the vulgarity of Mr. Bleet,
his occasional slips in grammar, the disagreeable condition of his half-melted vanilla ice.
Yes, the vanilla ice too contributes to the
reality and repulsiveness of Miss Dutton's
'tragedy'; insensibly we have grown as pre-
judiced as the neighbours.

We are unfair in more ways than one, for
there is no doubt that what most disgusts us,
most alienates our sympathy, is not Mr. Bleet's
wickedness, or supposed wickedness (after all
the vanilla ice is hardly evidence), but something ugly that surrounds and emanates from
him: it is as if this ugliness composed the greater
part of his sin, and all its horror. For sheer
suggestiveness I question if even *Seaton's Aunt*
surpasses this story. And its effect is the more
desolating because we dimly feel that Mr. Bleet
really is suffering in an inarticulate, incomplete
fashion (though certainly not suffering from
remorse), and that we *ought*, perhaps, to be
pitying instead of detesting him. If he were

quite without a soul, if he were not human, it would be so much simpler: it is the glimpses we get of that mis-shapen, hunted, jaunty yet abject spirit, that are so disquieting. After all, we don't really care a straw about Miss Dutton, who was vulgar, pretentious, and amorous. If she had forced her company upon *us*, and we could by a mere effort of will have caused her to be 'missing', 'missing' she infallibly would have been. So we bolster up our self-respect by casting fresh aspersions at Mr. Bleet. There is the disagreeable feature that he benefited financially by Miss Dutton's disappearance. And then—the ears—the glitter in the eyes—the powerful hairy hands. . . . It won't bear thinking about: we are not in the least like that. And it is the most appalling murder story ever written.

Let me turn, after this, if only for a moment, to a contemplation of the marvel of the writing; and there is a way in which I think it is more marvellous here than in any other of the stories. To explain what I mean I must mention the great difficulty that sometimes exists of adapting a highly individual style to realistic dialogue. I say 'sometimes', because for writers like Flaubert or Anatole France—writers whose

style, though completely individual, keeps
closely to the idiom of actual speech—the difficulty is at least greatly minimized. But for
Henry James in his last period, to take the most
extreme example I can think of, the difficulty was insurmountable. *Nobody* ever talked
(except possibly on occasion their author himself) as *everybody* talks in the later Jacobean
novels and stories. But they *had* to talk in
that way, they *had* to conform to the Jacobean
idiom and rhythm, otherwise each of their
remarks would have produced the distressing
effect of those sudden lapses into the spoken
phrase we find in old-fashioned opera. The
convention must be accepted as frankly as it
is accepted *in* opera, in the dialogues between
Tristan and Isolde. And though in the work
of Mr. de la Mare it is carried to nothing like
the same pitch, now and again here too we
must be prepared to accept it. It may be so
skilfully disguised that we don't notice it:
still the translation or adaptation is there.
Everything said by Mrs. Thripps (the charwoman in *Out of the Deep*), for instance, is true
to the mind and heart of Mrs. Thripps, but no
actual talk of a charwoman could possibly be
fitted just as it is into a de la Mare score. Mrs.

Thripps's words, if you examine them, you will find to have been recast. But the most subtle example of speech modulation I can think of is furnished by the talk of Mr. Bleet in this story, *Missing*, where it is managed so perfectly that we seem to be, and indeed *are*, listening to the very voice of the man, and yet listening to music. Miraculous as it may sound, vulgarity and commonness unutterable have lost not a shade of their identity, and yet are inseparable from beauty.

III

In the tales of the supernatural the realistic method is maintained, and what *can* be observed is shown with an unfailing mastery of description. Some feature in the scene evoked may even symbolize the kind of adventure that is to follow. The picture of the slimy pond swarming with tadpoles at the beginning of *Seaton's Aunt* is of this sort. It prepares us for the house we have not yet seen, but which is, in its turn, swarming with a kind of spiritual larvæ. All the material objects in *Seaton's Aunt* are solid, palpable, casting heavy shadows that somehow carry the imagination into regions of ghostly terror. In fact, in this particular story the only ghosts *are* these shadows—not so much as a glimpse of a vanishing apparition ever crosses the vision of either Seaton or his friend. What they see with their eyes is nothing more alarming than the Aunt herself, or her vast empty bed in 'the feeble clearness of a night-light': the whole drama emerges, deepens, darkens, in a succession of hints and omens. To this end the first appearance of Miss Seaton is masterly.

We were approaching the house when Seaton suddenly came to a standstill. Indeed, I have always had the impression that he plucked at my sleeve. Something, at least, seemed to catch me back, as it were, as he cried, 'Look out, there she is!'

She was standing at an upper window which opened wide on a hinge, and at first sight she looked an excessively tall and overwhelming figure. This, however, was mainly because the window reached all but to the floor of her bedroom. She was in reality rather an under-sized woman, in spite of her long face and big head. She must have stood, I think, unusually still, with eyes fixed on us, though this impression may be due to Seaton's sudden warning and to my consciousness of the cautious and subdued air that had fallen on him at sight of her. I know that without the least reason in the world I felt a kind of guiltiness, as if I had been 'caught'. There was a silvery star pattern sprinkled on her black silk dress, and even from the ground I could see the immense coils of her hair and the rings on her left hand which was held fingering the small jet buttons of her bodice. She watched our united advance without stirring, until, imperceptibly, her eyes raised and lost themselves in the distance, so that it was out of an assumed reverie that she appeared suddenly to awaken to our presence beneath her when we drew close to the house.

No more than this picture, but what a huge push forward it gives to the story. The uneasiness Miss Seaton inspires in the two schoolboys is contagious. It is heightened by the equivocal nature of its cause, and reaches its climax of sheer terror when they become aware that she is listening outside their bedroom door at night. But it is still more amazing, perhaps, how a sombre beauty flushes through this dreadful creation of a spiritual vampire, whose unnatural appetite has created a charnel-house atmosphere, the alluring reek of which has emptied the churchyard of its ghosts. Poor Withers's attempts—in self-defence—to take it all calmly, rationally—to regard Seaton's Aunt merely as a cynical, rather gross and greedy old lady with an unpleasant nephew and a disconcerting taste for ponderous irony—poor Withers's attempts, in short, to be an aloof little man of the world, are far from successful. Everything that happens is quite ordinary, or very nearly ordinary, and yet, as if by remorseless predestination, everything that happens

[219]

tends to the sinister. The first thing the boys
do when they reach the village where they are
to pass their half-term holiday with Miss Seaton
is to stop at a chemist's: 'We descended the
two steps into his dusky and odorous interior
to buy, I remember, some rat poison.' And a
little later they pause at the tadpole pond to
allow Seaton to examine his pets: 'I can see his
absorbed face now as he sat on his heels and fished
the slimy things out in his sallow palms.' Such
incidents are nothing when taken separately;
it is their cumulative effect that gets on
Withers's nerves. Even the room Miss Seaton
has allotted to him—the, at first sight, so 'jolly
little bedroom, with a brass fender and rugs
and a polished floor'—suddenly reveals the
peculiar 'touch' of his hostess. 'Over the wash-
stand was a little black-framed water-colour
drawing, depicting a large eye with an extremely fish-like intensity in the spark of light
on the dark pupil; and in "illuminated" letter-
ing beneath was printed very minutely, "Thou
God Seest ME", followed by a long looped
monogram, "S.S.", in the corner. . . . "This
is the room, Withers, my brother William died
in when a boy. Admire the view!"' The 'jolli-
ness', for poor Withers, dies out on the instant.

Seaton, as he stands that night in his pyjamas by his chum's dressing-table, supplies the finishing touch. ' "Even this room's nothing more than a coffin. I suppose she told you—'It's all exactly the same as when my brother William died'—trust her for that! And good luck to him, say I." '

There is something at once pathetic and repugnant about the nervous and furtive Seaton. He has the two qualities shared by all Mr. de la Mare's boys, of being at once strange and absolutely convincing. He has more pocket-money, larger hampers of food than his schoolfellows, and yet he dimly knows, and we know too, that he is doomed. He is exactly like a little rat swimming round and round in a water-trap, and we watch him growing feebler and feebler but still swimming, swimming, while his Aunt's big face leans in gloating interest over the abominable spectacle.

The thing is superbly done; the effect aimed at is that of terror, and this effect is achieved as elsewhere, I think, only in *The Turn of the Screw* and one or two stories by Edgar Poe. Everything contributes to it, from Miss Seaton's sarcasms to her nephew's behaviour at school:

everything, from the swarming tadpole pond
to the unfinished game of chess, is accepted by
the imagination as a symbol, and fulfils its
purpose.

One secret of the story's power lies in the
very absence from it of a visible ghost. I do
not mean that the effect of an apparition presented objectively need necessarily fall flat,
though the stories in which this sudden collapse
does *not* occur might be numbered on the
fingers of one hand. The ghost story, in truth,
if it is not merely to be crude and silly, demands
a very special technique quite beyond the reach
of the average concoctor of horrors. It is
significant that the only successful experiments
I can recall exhibit a marked element of beauty
—the last quality one would look for in sensational fiction. But in such things as *The Turn
of the Screw*, or Meade Falkner's *The Lost
Stradivarius*, the drama might very nearly be
described as a conflict between beauty and
ugliness. At all events, any fond idea that the
ghost in itself can constitute interest must result
in failure. The mere presence of a ghost,
decked in however grisly trappings, can only
interest the extremely artless. What may be
of the *intensest* interest, on the other hand, is

the presentation of a normal mind terrified, or revolted by, or simply struggling against the influence of, such an apparition. It is not the ghost but the person who sees the ghost that matters, therefore the finer the mind shown as reacting to such phenomena the richer will be our impression. *The Turn of the Screw* is the most moving and terrifying ghost story ever written simply because the *human* drama in it is the most poignant; and what would *Seaton's Aunt* be if the characters were the commonplace puppets of the ordinary 'thriller'?

In the de la Mare tales of the supernatural the effect aimed at is, characteristically, more lyrical than dramatic. From one of the most beautiful—*All Hallows*—drama is completely absent, and even in *Seaton's Aunt*, which probably is the best 'story as a story', there is no dramatic climax comparable to that in *The Turn of the Screw*. The concluding scene of *Seaton's Aunt* is a rounding-off of what has gone before: the tension is relaxed, it is pitched on a slightly lower key, and the end is brought about when the strings finally cease to vibrate; whereas in *The Turn of the Screw* they suddenly snap when emotion has reached its highest point, and the terrible cry of despair torn from the lost and dying boy still rings on in our ears after the book is closed.

In *Out of the Deep* (originally called *The Bell*) the ending is on the first page, and the story is told backwards. Here the hauntings actually materialize, impress themselves on sight, hearing, and even on the sense of smell. It is true that Jimmie's state of mind is abnormal. Disease and the ravages of a reckless life have broken down certain barriers, and it is because these barriers no longer exist that when he rings the bell in his empty house it is answered by such attendants. None the less, the implication remains that the attendants are real. They are not, I mean, to be taken as the visions of his fever, though Mrs. Thripps, the charwoman who comes in each day to tidy up and cook for him, can find no trace of their activities in the morning. Yet neither are they ordinary ghosts. The ghosts visiting Jimmie (dying lonely and disgraced in his hated Uncle's old house, even in his hated Uncle's 'prodigious yet elegant Arabian bed')—the ghosts, literally called up by him, have a relation to him on some mysterious spiritual plane, correspond to the moral condition of his mind at the moment when he tugs 'the sumptuous crimson pleated silk bell-pull'.

Jimmie is another example of the value of the human element in these excursions into the super-normal. His life has been deplorable. 'Even in his first breeches he was never what could be called a nice little boy.' But he has grown up since then, and the 'not-niceness' of thirty or so is a rather different matter from the 'not-niceness' of even the least desirable kind of little boy. For one thing it implies a whole world of experience the little boy at his worst can only be reaching out to; and this perhaps is why we are never placed on quite such intimate and confidential terms with Jimmie as we were with our Craftsman—why, when it comes to confidences, we return *to* his boyhood. An odious butler had been the bane of *his* early years too. Soames is more sanctimonious than Jacobs, but he is of the same kidney. 'Soames used frequently to wring Jimmie's then protuberant ears. Soames sneaked habitually; and with a sort of gloating piety on his drooping face, was invariably present at the subsequent castigation.' In a few pages the picture of a tarnished, loveless childhood is complete; its very comedy is tragic; and we watch that

P

shivering little wretch—obdurate, sullen, unhappy, an infallible liar—standing as if detected
in secret depravity while his Aunt Charlotte
reproves him for being 'so wickedly frightened
of the dark'. 'You know very well your dear
Uncle will not permit gas in the attic, so there's
no use asking for it. You have nothing on your
conscience, I trust?'

Aunt Charlotte might be forgiven much for
the sake of that remark; and she is nearer the
truth than she imagines, for poor Jimmie has
always had a good deal on his conscience and
always will have; but the small, flickering flame
of beauty in his spirit (without which he could
not be a de la Mare hero), of that Aunt
Charlotte and Uncle Timothy will never be
aware.

From tiny wandering seeds may spring marvellous plants, and from a sentence in a Welsh
Guide-Book, describing the situation by the sea
of St. David's Cathedral, sprang the tale of *All
Hallows*. The real St. David's (the outside of
which on inspection proved disappointing) was
not visited till after the story was written: the
whole thing therefore—story and scene—is the
creation of the writer.

All Hallows is not a ghost story; it is the account of an invasion by the powers of darkness of an ancient Christian stronghold now weakened through its garrison's lack of faith. The demons of the air, riding in from the sea on storm and cloud and mist, have found an entrance, and this once holy temple is being altered to their unholy purpose. Only the old sexton remains faithful, and it is he who tells the strange narrative to a sympathetic tourist, who, tired and dusty after a long tramp, finds himself towards the close of an August afternoon within the besieged precincts. *All Hallows* is a wonderful piece of writing. This cathedral not built of hands comes to life literally to the sound of music. Out of music it rises before us in its vastness and beauty, its wind-swept fairness. At first, with the weary grateful traveller, we simply gaze at it in admiration, rejoicing in its dream of quietness and beauty; and once only an uneasy question arises as to whether all is well. The momentary doubt is dismissed; but when the traveller has passed through a side door into the actual building, and finds himself suddenly listening to an incredible history, a vague fear begins to stir in the deepening twilight.

The grandeur remains, a sense of colossal yet delicate beauty, of wide spaces and the coolness and whiteness of sculptured stone. Unlike the tales of human hauntings, there is no ugliness here. The haunters have the dark majesty of fallen Angels and Principalities, and the two humans who spy on them are in comparison mere creeping things, safe so long as they hide themselves, do not come out into the open.

The traveller listens courteously; but what crazed, impossible secrets are these that are being poured into his ears! He is sceptical, curious, sympathetic—and gradually the narrative becomes less impossible, and then not impossible at all, as he becomes aware of evidence. Those great carved figures of saints that had looked so innocent from where he had first beheld them, as he emerges on the roof to a closer inspection reveal anything but saintly features and expressions. The work of alteration has not only begun but has proceeded far. And they must not linger too long, now that the light is failing: once—once the sexton had been nearly caught.

'In this very gallery. They nearly had me, sir. But by good fortune there's a recess a little further on—stored up with some old fragments of carving, from the original building, sixth-century, so it's said: stone capitals, heads and hands, and suchlike. I had had my warning, and managed to lep in there and conceal myself. But only just in time. Indeed, sir, I confess I was in such a condition of terror and horror I turned my back.'

'You mean, you heard, but didn't look? And—something came?'

'Yes, sir, I seemed to be reduced to no bigger than a child, huddled up there in that corner. There was a sound like clanging metal—but I don't think it was metal. It drew near at a furious speed, then passed me, making a filthy gust of wind. For some instants I couldn't breathe; the air was gone.'

'And no other sound?'

'No other sound, sir, except out of the distance a noise like the sounding of a stupendous kind of gibberish. A calling; or so it seemed—no human sound. The air shook with it. You see, sir, I myself wasn't of any consequence, I take it—unless a mere obstruction in the way. But—I have heard it said somewhere that the rarity of these happenings is only because it's a pain and torment and not any sort of pleasure for such beings, such apparitions, sir, good or bad, to visit our outward world.'

It is evident that a story like this must either succeed or utterly fail: there can be no half measures, because the drop from the sublime to the ridiculous—or shall I in this case say to the merely sensational?—is precipitous. *All Hallows*, to my mind, succeeds. The achievement is worthy of the conception, and leaves in memory that sense of a unique and beautiful

[229]

experience which is produced more frequently by a fine poem than by fiction.

The Green Room is less striking in theme, and at first sight may appear to be in the tradition of the ordinary ghost story. In two respects, indeed it is: the apparition appears in the accustomed way, and the young man who sees it is unimportant. Alan is a naïve and pleasant but rather colourless youth, his only claim to distinction being a certain delicacy of feeling. It might be argued that he is at least as interesting as the humans in *All Hallows*, but then the humans in *All Hallows* hardly count, the cathedral itself is the hero of that composition, and in a way that certainly cannot be claimed for the second-hand bookshop which is the scene of *The Green Room*. What the story does express, and very pleasantly, is a fragile, lingering, half-pathetic sense of the past. Moreover, there is something ghostly in the very weakness and futility of Alan's frail and damaged wraith; but it is pity, not fear, she arouses even in him. Just for a moment perhaps there is horror—in a veiled and terrible suggestion of an appetite existing beyond the grave. But it is no more than a hint, the dramatization of *that* particular idea would have led to a very different tale.

Alan's ghost is the phantom of a woman betrayed and deserted, one whom suffering did not ennoble, and who eventually committed suicide. Once she had lived in this very house where the shop is—lived here in a relationship that remains undefined with a certain Dr. Marchmont. Dr. Marchmont, whether lover or brother, belonged to the last, unrecorded phase of her life; and we get just a tiny glimpse of what that household may have been from a few books left behind—books of the kind described in catalogues as 'curious'. The lady herself left a manuscript volume of verses in the manner of Acton Bell, but commemorating an experience Acton would never have commemorated. Alan at any rate finds the verses, and with them a photograph—not of his ghost, but of what she once had been in the days of innocence. That the innocence was lost, and possibly even derided, is revealed gradually to him—the full, shocking understanding only coming when, after he has had her verses printed, he learns that this sentimental kindness is not in the least what she really wants of him. It is all, as I say, hinted rather than stated, with infinite subtlety and ingenuity. The quoted verses themselves are a marvel of ingenuity, of the gift of getting outside one's own skin and into that of a completely different person.

As a story, *The Green Room* produces no such electrical effect as *Seaton's Aunt* and some of the other tales. It is very quiet, and I should hesitate to say that the last drop of intensity had been squeezed out of the strange situation. For *that*, I rather think, it would have been necessary to have faced the uncompromisingly unpleasant, and had he done so Mr. de la Mare could not have kept his story in tone with the delicate, slightly faded colouring of the old-fashioned room, with the scent of antique bindings and the fairness of black type on ancient pages, which all through it has been his aim to do.

The reader who would sup on horrors must turn to *A Recluse*—the nearest approach to a 'shocker' the author ever wrote. By this I mean that if it scares us it has fulfilled all its purpose. Far be it from me to breathe a word against such a purpose. It is not the highest, but only a pedant or a prig will deny that he enjoys being thrilled, and our superior attitude towards sensational fiction is adopted largely because the blat**ant and** the crude *fail* to produce this effect. The method in *A Recluse* is akin to the method in *Seaton's Aunt*, but the result is different. The strangeness is here, but somehow not the beauty. And yet the material used is no uglier than the material used in several tales—in *Missing*, for example, or *An Ideal Craftsman*: it is simply that it has not undergone the spiritual transmutation we find in these stories—is used to a different end: there is no conflict between beauty and ugliness; nothing, as it were, to mark the spiritual values; the story is launched directly at our nerves.

And it succeeds: we can trust Mr. de la Mare's skill for that: the horror thrusts through, though I am doubtful if anything else does, if there *is* anything else, and we cannot be blamed if our author has taught us to look for more. Mr. Bloom, at all events, is an acquaintance who will not quickly be forgotten. He is a spiritualist who has carried things rather far —to a point, in fact, when those whom he has been accustomed to summon no longer wait to be summoned. Mr. Bloom emphatically is *there*; and, more unaccountably, so to a great extent is the young man, now deceased, who was his secretary, though of him we are shown nothing but his clothes and the aspect of his bedroom, which Mr. Bloom's reluctant guest for one night only wakes up to take due stock of. The effect is distinctly gruesome; the whole tale is gruesome—so much and so *physically* so that we quite understand and share the guest's loss of appetite when he sits down to the tempting supper provided for him. Ugliness somehow exudes from everything remotely connected with Mr. Bloom (from his rare old furniture and Waterford glass to his chickens in their white sauce and all the other baked meats provided at that ample and faintly disgusting feast), or rather it exudes from Mr. Bloom himself, and rests on his possessions like the smear of a greasy hand.

But the story reaches our nerves, grips us closely even while some of its ramifications are not clearly grasped. Our first suspicion, for instance, when Mr. Bloom by tampering with his unwilling visitor's car, tricks him into spending a night at Montrésor—our first suspicion that he wants him for some sinister experiment, proves mistaken. Yet if Mr. Bloom *merely* was terrified at the thought of spending a night alone in Montrésor (his own house, which he is preparing to leave), surely we should be given a very cogent reason for his being obliged to do so: as it is, there seems to have been nothing to prevent him from leaving the house in the afternoon and returning to it next morning. Nor is the climax of the story quite clear: I mean the scene where the visitor, waking at dawn and hearing strange noises overhead, goes to Mr. Bloom's room.

What I was not prepared for was the spectacle of Mr. Bloom's bed. When I entered the room, I am perfectly certain there had been nothing abnormal about that—except that it had not been slept in. True, the light had meanwhile increased a little, but not much. No—the bed had been empty.

Not so now. The lower part of it was all but entirely flat, the white coverlid over it was drawn almost as neat and close from side to side of it as the cover of a billiard table. But on the pillow, the beard protruding over the turned-down sheet, now showed what appeared to be the head and face of Mr. Bloom. With head jerked back, I watched that face steadily, transfixedly. It was a flawless facsimile, waxen, motionless; but it was not a real face and head. It was an hallucination. How induced is quite another matter. No spirit of life, no livingness had ever stirred those soap-like, stagnant features. . . . It was merely a mask, a life-like mask (past even the dexterity of a Chinese artist to rival), and—though I hardly know why—it was inconceivably shocking.

Well, we know why it is shocking. It is because it is ugly—so ugly that it becomes

[235]

obscene. It is meant to shock, and it succeeds; but what *is* this counterfeit Mr. Bloom?

It may be that I do wrong to criticize *A Recluse*, for as yet it has been published only in Lady Cynthia Asquith's *Ghost Book* of 1926. I pass therefore the more readily to *Miss Jemima*, which, though it is the slightest of all these tales, is definitely in the first rank. I have detached it from the collection of children's stories called *Broomsticks* where it is placed, because, though it too certainly is a children's story, the author here believes every word he writes. It is a story told to a little girl called Susan by her granny, and the relation between this happily assorted pair contributes an exquisitely domestic charm to what is really a narrative of spiritual danger. When Susan's granny was a little girl she was very nearly lured beyond the boundary we are forbidden to pass; only the merest chance saved her, a single tiny peep, coming just not too late, into the true nature of the lovely being who wanted her.

Miss Jemima is so delightful a thing, so essentially fine and true, that to mention Susan's two 'exacalys' and her one 'quincidence' as having aroused a momentary uneasiness goes very much against the grain. All the rest of Susan's conversation is beautifully right—which is just the reason why I *do* mention these doubtful locutions. Susan, indeed, may have used them, though children even at the age of six or seven (and she is older than that) are generally absurdly pedantic about the pronunciation of a long or unfamiliar word. It probably doesn't—the word, I mean—always come right, but on the other hand, in my experience, it rarely if ever comes in the manner of Susan's 'exacalys' and Ann's 'stremelys' (Ann of *Crossings*), possibly because individuals have individual tricks of speech, and these are established literary forms. Whether right or wrong, however, was not quite my point. When I said that these speeches aroused uneasiness, it was because they seemed to me to constitute an appeal—such as we do not expect from Mr. de la Mare. He never makes that appeal when he is writing about little boys: them we have to take on their merits be they never so slender.

IV

Through these two girls, Susan and Ann, we reach our third group of stories, in which I include *Crossings*, though it is written in dramatic form. That beautiful play of ghosts and fairies, butchers, bakers and candlestick-makers, must have been conceived and carried out in a singularly happy mood. It is a blend of magic, fun, and poetry, and its setting is a world of dusk and silver, where houses, woods, and people are all exactly as we should like them to be. If I place it in Group Three, indeed, it is only because there is no symbol in its dreaming; all belongs frankly to 'once-upon-a-time'. The plot is fantasy. The children escape from a grim Bayswater Aunt, and in the country, at Crossings,—an old house with a ghost and a mouse or two—live for a while by themselves; and the youngest child, Ann, is stolen by fairies and brought back again.

I am completely ignorant of the problems of dramatic production, but it seems to me *Crossings* would present far fewer difficulties in its actual mounting than, say, *The Blue Bird*, while the play itself is infinitely fresher and more charming. There might be some trouble in finding an Ann, but so long as the schoolboy brother was not represented by a plump little person bulging out of her Etons in curves fatal to illusion we could accept an Ann older than the author's portrait, and all the rest would be plain sailing.

At any rate, as a poem, as a story, as an arm-chair drama, the thing is exquisite. It is fooling of course, lovely midsummer night's fooling, but the touch is so deft, the spirit so gravely humorous and tender, that at the time we take it half seriously. The very fact that the characters are so much de la Mare characters, the house so much a de la Mare house, gives it, as a play, the rarest charm of familiarity in strangeness.

And several of the fairy tales proper—*The Dutch Cheese*, *The Sleeping Boys of Warwickshire*, *The Lovely Myfanwy*, to pick out two or three examples—are also first-rate things of their kind. It is not a kind wholly suited to Mr. de la Mare. The fairy tale (and it must be remembered I am speaking now of the old-fashioned fairy tale of Perrault and Grimm) depends for success almost as much on ingenuity of plot as does the mystery story. The plot must have a beginning, middle, and end, and the end must come in the nature of a surprise, a climax, the excitement must be steadily progressive. Certainly the three stories by Mr. de la Mare I have mentioned fulfil these conditions, but there are others which do not. *Wages*, for instance, an attempt in the same genre, appears to me not so much a story as a group of incidents for a story which has still to be invented. In both *Wages* and *John Cobler* (they will be found in the *Joy Street* annuals), after an excellent start the tale carries on for a little; then gradually loses its momentum, and ceases languidly. As for that long Hoffmannesque fantasy, *A Nose*, even the beginning seems to me unpromising. I may be advertising my own heaviness, but I confess I see nothing amusing in the idea of a person growing up from childhood in the belief his nose is made of wax: at any rate it is not in this kind of thing that we need look for the true quality of our author.

The children's stories that are really his, and which I would place in my last group, strike an entirely different note. It is the old difference, I suppose, between fancy and imagination. *Maria Fly*, *Visitors*, *Alice's Godmother*, *Broomsticks*: from such tales all the ingredients of the traditional fairy tale are conspicuously absent. They are not dependent on plot (at least not on any ingeniously arranged plot), they depend on the quality of the imagination in them—the imagination that creates reality. So, with our little friend Maria Fly: 'On purpose she didn't even glance again at the Fly. She most particularly (though she didn't know why) wished not to see it again. So she walked sidelong a little, her head turned to one side, too, so that no part of her eye should see the fly again even by accident.' Those sentences have very much the value of the picture of Seaton hovering over his pond of tadpoles. They have, indeed, an effect less startling than, but not dissimilar in kind from that of the sudden clear ringing of a telephone bell in the dead stillness of night. They create instantly an alertness: create, too, that reality—however far removed from normal experience—I have spoken of as characteristic of all Mr. de la Mare's most authentic work.

The line of division, in fact, between the best of these children's tales, and stories like *The Creatures*, *The Tree*, or even *The Vats*, is of a gossamer thinness: we might say the latter would be unlikely to appeal to a child, but that is all. I choose these three so different compositions because their underlying theme is an old de la Mare theme—more or less disguised in the two first, but in *The Vats* expressed

directly, if whimsically; and with the un-
hurried gravity of a bygone century echoing
in the elaborate imagery and full, solemn chords
of its prose.

We had frittered away, squandered so many days, weeks,
years—and had saved so little. Spendthrifts of the unborrow-
able, we had been living on our capital—a capital bringing
in how meagre an 'interest'—and were continually growing
poorer. Once, when we were children, and in our own
world, an hour had been as capacious as the blue bowl of the
sky, and of as refreshing a milk. Now its successors hag-
gardly snatched their way past our sluggard senses like thieves
pursued. . . .

We came at once to a standstill amid the far-flung stretches
of the unknown plateau on which we had re-found ourselves,
and with eyes fixed upon these astonishing objects, stood
and stared. I have called them Vats. Vats they were not;
but rather sunken Reservoirs; vast semi-spherical primeval
Cisterns. . . . They wore that air of lovely timelessness
which decks the thorn, and haunts for the half-woken sense
the odour of sweet-briar; yet they were grey with the ever-
lasting, as are the beards of the patriarchs and the cindery
craters of the Moon. Theirs was the semblance of having
been lost, forgotten, abandoned, like some foundered Nereid-
haunted derelict of the first sailors, rotting in dream upon
an undiscovered shore. They haunched their vast shapes
out of the green beneath the sunless blue of space, and for
untrodden leagues around them stretched like a paradisal
savanna what we poor thronging clock-vexed men call
Silence. Solitude. . . .

They called to mind some hidden being within us that,
if not their coeval, was at least aware of their exquisite
antiquity. Whether of archangelic or daemonic construc-

tion, clearly they had remained unvisited by mortal man for as many centuries at least as there are cherries in Damascus or beads in Tierra del Fuego. . . . Yet within the lightless bellies of these sarcophagi were heaped up, we were utterly assured (though *how*, I know not) floods, beyond measure, of the waters for which our souls had pined. Waters imaginably so clear as to be dense, as if of melted metal more translucent even than crystal; of such a tenuous purity that not even the moonlit branches of a dream would spell their reflex in them; so costly, so far beyond price, that this whole stony world's rubies and sapphires and amethysts of Mandalay and Guadalajara and Solikamsk, all the treasure-houses of Cambalech and the booty of King Tamburlane would suffice to purchase not one drop.

CHAPTER XII

CONCLUSION

I HAVE reached the end of my notes. In them prose has been separated from verse, novels from short stories, and the stories themselves divided into groups, yet looking back over Mr. de la Mare's work from the beginning, I become more than ever aware that these divisions are formal. Henry Brocken ambling gently along on Rosinante through the land of other dreamer's dreams; Nod skipping happily through the enchanted forests of Munza-Mulgar; Arthur Lawford wandering in that unmapped country where the lights from two worlds meet and struggle for mastery: such themes point to an imagination that dwells perpetually on one plane. The aim of these prose works is similar to that of the poems; the degree of their accomplishment may vary, but always (and in *The Midget*, too, this is so) their purpose is to weave the dream fabric so real to the author into the solid substance of actuality.

CONCLUSION

It is possible that a rarer and higher beauty is attained in the verse (indeed it cannot be denied that in some of the tales there is a perceptible thickening of the atmosphere), but when we say this are we not thinking of certain lyrics in the later poetry books, and therefore have we not an equal right to select passages from the prose in which this rarest, highest beauty also shines clear? It would be possible to do so. In both prose and verse a world is created markedly different from the world of fact, though not detached from it, and in spite of many strangenesses neither extravagant nor difficult of access. It is lit by heavenly, and often ghostly lights, but it is at the same time intensely human. And each successive book, whether in prose or verse, opened a door into it, though usually into a new and unexplored part.

Am I, by saying this, circumscribing the range of subject-matter within too narrow an area? It is limited, but with the passing of years we have seen the horizon pushed farther and farther back. I am really only referring to a singleness of vision that has always seen all life as a spiritual quest and adventure. There is no monotony. For the purpose of

this essay I re-read the entire work in poetry
and prose, and, though I was approaching
nothing for the first time, my impression was
of a constant freshness and variety, a constant
element of surprise. Things recur: themes—
treated with a difference; a certain favourite
physical type; certain humours and idiosyncrasies; a few favourite images and landscapes.
But image and picture at least are the symbols
every poet uses, and they have this symbolic
value in the prose and verse of Mr. de la Mare.

> Breathe not—trespass not,
> Of this green and darkling spot,
> Latticed from the moon's beams,
> Perchance a distant dreamer dreams;
> Perchance upon its darkening air,
> The unseen ghosts of children fare,
> Faintly swinging, sway and sweep,
> Like lovely sea-flowers in the deep;
> While, unmoved, to watch and ward,
> Amid its gloomed and daisied sward,
> Stands with bowed and dewy head
> That one little leaden Lad.

The landscape is always spiritualized, becomes a changeless, eternal landscape of the
soul. There are old churchyards, and old
gardens, with green sunken walks and trees
spreading mossy and lichened boughs above

them. There are dark old houses, with the wind sighing through their key-holes, and perhaps, from an upper casement, a face looking 'out of sorcery'. There are the burning fires of frost and stars, and black ice-bound winter pools, and frozen snow marked by the rabbit's 'tell-tale footprints'. There are birds hovering within vision, yet singing out of a molten glory of Paradise.

In this poetry, this prose, the unseen world is more constantly present than it is in the work of any other English poet perhaps, except Blake. Yet there is no likeness to Blake; an occasional spiritual affinity—and I have already mentioned such affinities with Emily Brontë, with Poe, with Vaughan and Traherne. Beneath everything there is that human undertone, a fineness of spirit, an attitude of mind composed of tenderness and kindness and understanding. It is too frequently overlooked in the eagerness to do justice to the glamour of a more supernatural beauty, but without it there could not be that moral and spiritual beauty which springs as much from the heart as from the imagination, and which seems to me, in the case of Mr. de la Mare, to be the rarest, the most endearing and precious gift of all.

And so I leave it, conscious that it is difficult to praise quite freely the genius of a living writer, at least when that writer is a friend of many years; conscious, too, that the influence of poetry is a spiritual influence, and must therefore remain incalculable.

September 1928
January 1929

LIST OF BOOKS
BY WALTER DE LA MARE

Songs of Childhood.   Longmans, Green & Co.   1902.
Henry Brocken.   John Murray.   1904.
Poems.   John Murray.   1906.
The Three Mulla-Mulgars.   Duckworth & Co.   1910.
The Return.   Edward Arnold.   1910.
The Listeners and Other Poems.   Constable & Co.   1912.
A Child's Day.   Constable & Co.   1912.
Peacock Pie: A Book of Rhymes.   Constable & Co.   1913.
Songs of Childhood (First Revised Edition).   1916.
The Sunken Garden.   Beaumont Press.   1917.
Motley and Other Poems.   Constable & Co.   1918.
Flora.   William Heinemann.   1919.
Rupert Brooke and the Intellectual Imagination.   Sidgwick &
    Jackson.   1919.
Poems 1901–1918.   Constable & Co.   1920.
Crossings: A Fairy Play.   Beaumont Press.   1921.
The Veil and Other Poems.   Constable & Co.   1921.
Memoirs of a Midget.   W. Collins Sons & Co.   1921.
Story and Rhyme.   J. M. Dent & Sons.   1921.
Down-Adown-Derry: A Book of Fairy Poems.   Constable &
    Co.   1922.
Thus Her Tale.   Porpoise Press.   1923.
The Riddle and Other Stories.   Selwyn & Blount.   1923.
Lispet, Lispett and Vaine.   'The Bookman's Journal'.
    1923.
Come Hither.   Constable & Co.   1923.

WALTER DE LA MARE

Some Thoughts on Reading.   Yellowsands Press.   1923.

Ding Dong Bell.   Selwyn & Blount.   1924.

A Ballad of Christmas.   Selwyn & Blount.   1924.

Christmas.   Selwyn & Blount.   1925.

Two Tales.   'The Bookman's Journal'.   1925.

Miss Jemima.   Basil Blackwell.   1925.

Broomsticks and Other Tales.   Constable & Co.   1925.

The Connoisseur and Other Stories.   W. Collins & Co.
   1926.

Alone.   Faber & Gwyer.   1927.

Told Again.   Basil Blackwell.   1927.

Stuff and Nonsense.   Constable & Co.   1927.

Self to Self.   Faber & Gwyer.   1928.

The Captive and Other Poems.   The Bowling Green Press.
   1928.

At First Sight.   Crosby Gaige.   1928.

Stories from the Bible.   Faber & Gwyer.   1929.

INDEX

[251]

INDEX

INDEX

[253]

INDEX

INDEX

INDEX